VICTORIAN CRITICAL INTERVENTIONS
Donald E. Hall, Series Editor

T0158294

PERSPECTIVES

*Modes of Viewing and Knowing
in Nineteenth-Century England*

Linda M. Shires

THE OHIO STATE UNIVERSITY PRESS

Columbus

Library of Congress Cataloging-in-Publication Data
Shires, Linda M., 1950–
   Perspectives : modes of viewing and knowing in nineteenth-century England / Linda M. Shires.
      p. cm. — (Victorian critical interventions)
  Includes bibliographical references and index.
  ISBN-13: 978-0-8142-1097-0 (cloth : alk. paper)
  ISBN-10: 0-8142-1097-X (cloth : alk. paper)
  1. English poetry—19th century—History and criticism—Theory, etc. 2. Literature and society—England—History—19th century. 3. Optics in literature. 4. Photography in literature. 5. Subjectivity in literature. 6. Objectivity in literature. I. Title.
  PR595.O6P47 2009
  821'.8093552—dc22

                      2008051411

This book is available in the following editions:
Paper (ISBN: 978-0-8142-5753-1)
Cloth (ISBN 978-0-8142-1097-0)
CD-ROM (ISBN 978-0-8142-9193-1)

Cover design by Dan O'Dair.
Text design and typesetting by Jennifer Shoffey Forsythe.
Type set in Adobe Palatino.

For U. C. Knoepflmacher
and in memory of E. D. H. Johnson

CONTENTS

ILLUSTRATIONS

Figure 1

D. G. Rossetti, *The Girlhood of Mary Virgin*, 1848–49.
Oil on canvas, 83.2 x 65.4 cm. Tate Gallery, London. • 37

Figure 2

Henry Peach Robinson, "Fading Away,"
composite photograph made from five negatives, 1858;
George Eastman Collection, Rochester, New York. • 66

Figure 3

Lady Clementina Hawarden, "Clementina Maude,"
photographed at 5 Princes Gardens, South Kensington, London.
About 1862–63; Albumen print from wet collodion negative.
Victoria and Albert Photography Department, London. Museum no.
PH.457:344-1968. • 81

ACKNOWLEDGMENTS

I am especially grateful to colleagues and friends who helped me refine points and who generously answered inquiries. Warm thanks go to those who read all or parts of this manuscript: Bob Gates, Steve Weiss, and Mike Goode. The Syracuse University English Department 2007–2008 Faculty Writing group afforded evenings of welcome intellectual exchange during a long winter and spring. Although I have moved to a new university position, these insightful former colleagues know that my warm wishes remain with them: Susan Edmunds, Claudia Klaver, Patty Roylance, Roger Hallas, Monika Wadman, Jeannie Britton, and Vincent Stephens. A lively conversation in New York City with E. Warwick Slinn about a range of nineteenth-century poems came late in the going, but at a crucial moment, nonetheless.

Steven Cohan supported me more like a brother than a friend during the writing of this book. Since he retains everything I don't—from numerous facts (like what is covered on my insurance policies), to our old co-authored manuscript pages from *Telling Stories*, to all the books I sold many years ago and then needed again off his bookshelves—his help proved essential on more than one occasion. While busy writing on twentieth-century film and television, he nevertheless offered a sympathetic ear about texts in which he had only a remote interest.

My extraordinary husband, Uli, exercised his usual care in watering the seeds of ideas and in reading first drafts—using the motif of the long, skinny dachshund, in red pen, for those sentences which seemed to go on way too long or to have lost themselves in a neighboring yard. I won't easily forget our excited conversations about Rossetti and Dyce, our visit together to the fantastic Turner retrospective at the Metropolitan Museum of Art, his single parenting for a year, or that beach vacation, dangling before me if I would just finish the revisions. Our son Alex had nothing to do with the book; he wisely kept his perspective focused on his social life and his own intellectual and creative pursuits as he headed to college.

The Victorians Institute, the MLA, The Society for Textual Studies, and the North American Victorian Studies Association offered valuable venues to present material on word and image to specialized audiences. John Maynard, Jim Kincaid, Susan Wolfson, Pamela Dalziel, Nick Frankel, Patricia Ingham, Esther Schor, Amy Lang, and Lorraine Janzen Kooistra answered specific queries, helped with sources, offered opportunities to speak, or otherwise lent support. Roslyn Vanderbilt, Ruth Bennett, Holly Nelson, and Ken Pallack shared coffee, poems, stories and time. I also thank my mother, Helen Shires, for her interest in things academic, at a time when her own concerns were far more pressing.

During 2006–2007, Cathryn Newton, Dean of the College of Arts and Sciences, and Professor Gregg Lambert, Chair, Department of English at Syracuse University, provided me with research and administrative leave. I am grateful for a generous contribution towards illustration permissions from Dean Gerald Greenberg. Because of the high reproduction costs for color illustrations, especially for an academic press, I have set up a website at www.lindashires.com which features many of the paintings and photographs referenced in this book. As this book went to press, my editors and I discovered that the Victoria and Albert Museum has made obtaining reproductions far easier and less expensive than in the past, for which we were grateful.

For three years, Kevin Mensch has made my online days in Firestone Library, Princeton University, run smoothly. Two anonymous readers for The Ohio State University Press made salient suggestions I have worked to address fully. I could not have been luckier in my editors: Sandy Crooms of The Ohio State University Press and Donald E. Hall, series editor, who showed eager initial interest and patient long-term support.

This book provides an opportunity to celebrate the careers of two of Princeton University's outstanding scholars of nineteenth-century literature and culture: my husband, U. C. Knoepflmacher, and his mentor, the late E. D. H. Johnson. It is offered as a modest token of gratitude for their superb teaching and writing, which opened new vistas for numerous students, colleagues, and friends over the years.

Princeton, NJ and New York, NY, February 2009

INTRODUCTION

But besides holding your head still, you must, when you try to trace the picture on the glass, shut one of your eyes. If you do not, the point of the brush appears double. . . . Perspective can, therefore, only be quite right, by being calculated for one fixed position of the eye of the observer; nor will it ever appear deceptively right unless seen precisely from the point it is calculated for. Custom, however, enables us to feel the rightness of the work on using both our eyes, and to be satisfied with it, even when we stand at some distance from the point it is designed for.
—John Ruskin, The Elements of Perspective *(1859), 241–42*

To say that our culture has been and continues to be shaped, informed and pro-grammed at bedrock level by the perspective paradigm is more than wordplay—though language requires that perspective not be an object like any other, because, metaphorically speaking, it has a bearing on the conditions determinant of all objectivity, of perception of objects, from whatever angle or point of view they might be considered in relation to a horizon line or a set distance.
—Hubert Damisch, The Origin of Perspective *(1995), 52*

Written while he was teaching art to young girls at Winnington Hall School, John Ruskin's manual on perspective, quoted above, was meant to be read in conjunction with the first three books of Euclid. No doubt, his appreciation for geometry as well as art and "right" seeing fueled his interest in writing and illustrating such a book. How useful it may have been to schoolgirls sketching landscapes or to amateurs learning to draw cathedrals in scenic views is another matter. Still, Ruskin firmly believed that all artists should learn the basic rules of Renaissance linear perspective, distance, horizon line, and standing point. He bemoaned the fact that few painters knew the complexity of the rules, and fewer still followed them. Even his favorite painter, J. M. W. Turner, though appointed Professor of Perspective at the Royal Academy years before executing his later, most abstract paintings, knew nothing, Ruskin maintained, about perspective.

This interdisciplinary book reopens the question of classical perspective and its vicissitudes in aesthetic practice from the 1830s through the 1870s in England.[1] The impulse to tackle such a demanding and slippery concept as *perspective* emerged from my study of Victorian poetry, particularly the dramatic monologue and double poem. These innovative Victorian poetic forms, reconceiving the relationship between subject and object, caused me to question how and why both the visual and verbal texts of the nineteenth century came to be more widely created (if not always received) as self-conscious and skeptical representations. What relationship might there be among a growing secularization, the creation of novels and long narrative poems involving double narratives and multiple tellers, and the shifting fortunes of a transcendental "I" in poetry and a mastering eye in painting or photography? Did not art forms, as much as new technologies and the rise of science, educate readers and viewers into new ways of knowing? And, most importantly, what do nineteenth-century literary and visual texts themselves have to say about modes of viewing and knowing, not entirely through theme, but through their forms? Might we maintain that the verbal and visual are separate languages (Mitchell 1994), yet theorize a relationship between them that pivots on perspective and point of view, particularly in an increasingly ocularcentric Western culture? While I would not claim perspective to be the key to all mythologies, it is an especially important concept to unravel because, while most pertinent to optics and the history of vision, it comes to us mediated by metaphor and thus inflects art history and literary history with questions of epistemology.

The scholarly answers available to my questions did not satisfy me, nor did the frequent focus by critics on one genre to the exclusion of others. Although Victorian poetry, in particular, has often been studied in formal terms by itself, nineteenth-century verbal texts are mutually intertextual and, even more important, mutually imbricated with visual texts in social and cultural formations transcending specific genres, modes, or discourses. For some time, I have advocated an interdisciplinary study which explores issues across genres and not only pertaining to poet-painters. In connecting the concepts of visual perspective with literary point of view, and exploring nineteenth-century examples of both, I am purposefully bridging seemingly separate realms of art.

Much important work has been conducted on vision and the nineteenth century over the past twenty years (Kemp; Flint; Crary 1992 and 2001; Christ and Jordan). Not surprisingly, technology and science, including the science of optics itself, play a role in a narrative of influence (Crary 1992). The central technology of photography has been credited with shaping novel form (N. Armstrong) and impacting Pre-Raphaelite and fin de siècle women's poetry (L. Smith; A. Vadillo). Conflicting nineteenth-century discourses about photography have been connected to realism and romance (Green-Lewis) and to nonfictional prose and lyric (L. Smith; Groth)—to different ends. While I agree with many of the details of these and other specific studies, technology is only one of many forces shaping permutations in aesthetic form. It should not be privileged alone as a cultural force, so that it comes to seem deterministic. Moreover, as Mirzoeff suggests, any neat parallel between scientific advances and visual representations simply does not hold up to close scrutiny (1999, 38).

Critics studying interconnections between visual art and literature who are not concerned with science or technology, usually focus on thematic connections or on how the pictorial shapes various art forms (Meisel; Andres). While we have separate studies of literary point of view and visual perspective, the task of analyzing varied art forms of the same period in terms of their experimentation with classical linear perspective and realist point of view has not, to my knowledge, been attempted. Moreover, in looking for innovative or experimental forms, critics usually favor the end of the period as the prelude to Modernism and cinema. In so doing, they follow the stereotypical rupture narratives about modernity—whether in terms of science (Einstein's theory of relativity and the destruction of pictorial space in cubism) or literary form (the advent of stream of consciousness, imagism, and alterations to subjectivity and objectivity) or the history of the gaze (the flâneur, window shopping, the glance and new mobilities in new spaces).

Those intellectual historians locating formal innovation in the late nineteenth century and early twentieth have insisted on "delayed artistic repercussions" to the waning influence of geometric optics (Jay 1996, 97). Many have supported the stereotypical view of Victorian art and aesthetics, summarized by Rachel Teukolsky recently as: "sentimental, moralizing, and straitlaced," a view, moreover, "cemented by British modernists, whose violent rejection of their predecessors made it difficult to see beyond the twentieth-century caricatures of these figures" (712). While Teukolsky's summary is admittedly reductive, used for heuristic purposes, it retains enough truth to indicate that we need to review freshly how we read Victorian texts and how we view Victorian artworks.

This book offers analyses of individual texts and raises questions that will hopefully help move us further in that direction. First, isn't there a more nuanced explanation for the history of perspective than the "waning of geometric optics," which is based in a teleological and developmental model? Second, could we not insist that experimentation with optics and perspective in the visual arts, at least, occurred from the Renaissance (see Elkins 1994) right through modernism and beyond? Moreover, the mimetic and metaphoric uses of perspective mean that these dimensions are historically related and conceptually similar, but not identical. There is a looseness built into the perspectival paradigm and its meanings from the beginning.

Unlike critics who argue for delayed artistic repercussions in the late nineteenth century or who still support the now discredited modernism rupture theory, I contend that influential writers and artists experimented with varied techniques for perspective in the early to mid-nineteenth century. Their work should not be overlooked as part of a continuing historical process of often coexisting models and paradigms for seeing and knowing. The nineteenth-century cultural texts I examine experiment with types of perspective, while questioning any unmediated, objective, single, or easily won consensual "truth" purported by linear perspective or classic realism in visual or verbal art, respectively.

This book demonstrates that the cultural revaluation of the relationship of subject to object taking place from the 1830s through the 1870s, via experiments with perspective, can be located across visual and verbal media—from painting to poetry to photography to fiction. As Ruskin's comment above indicates, and as many artists and writers of the time well understood, vision is intimately bound up with the physiological space of the viewer and all his or her senses, as well as with habits and ideological assumptions that go beyond the mathematical "sureties" of geometry or of a disembodied, fixed-gaze, camera obscura model. It is not that Turner did not know perspective, but that it was far less interesting to him than other ways the eye organizes objects and sees them.

The linear perspective paradigm, however, based as it is in stable, reassuring, single-point perspective, continued to exert a dominant sway in culture—maintaining accustomed ways of looking and of knowing, as Damisch states in my second epigraph.[2] Given its metaphoric links to naturalism and realism, this "Enlightenment invention" remained a major paradigm for modern vision and thought.[3] Our ideas about unified pictorial space and reality, via Alberti's metaphor of the transparent window as a frame for perspectival views, run very deep (see Friedberg 2006). Despite the complications and subversions introduced by artists and critics, the geometric organizing of distance and of objects in space remains central to our modern, Western cultural imagination. The persistent importance of Renaissance perspective and its elevation to an explanatory model in varied systems of thought stem from its accessibility as a system of projection that allows us to think we have knowledge about the world that we apprehend. On the one hand, it makes the world intelligible; on the other hand, it seems to duplicate the real (see Moxley, Melville 1990, and Elkins online work in progress, 5).[4]

Therefore, this book maintains that Renaissance perspective did not simply disappear in the early nineteenth century through a growing psychologization of vision and loss of belief in the truth of the eye, but that it remained as a popular and sometimes still dominant force in the visual and verbal arts. At the same time, as the visual field expanded, alternative models of vision and of the viewer developed side by side. The shift from a single, seemingly objective, universal perspective to an increasing preoccupation with the processes of perception produced an experimentation with flattening, dissolution, and combination in the visual arts, and multiplicity of perspective in the verbal arts. In questioning how we see and know, such experiments inevitably reworked the key elements of perspectival vision: fixity, space, the relationship of subject and object, veracity.

DEFINITION—WHAT IS CLASSIC LINEAR PERSPECTIVE?

As a term relating to vision and geometry, perspective refers to a system for representing visible objects in three-dimensional space on the surface or in two dimensions of a picture. By keeping one eye open and one shut, as Ruskin suggests, seeing in perspective is monocular, with all the focus and the limits that term implies. *Perspective* derives from the Latin *perspicere*, meaning to see clearly, to look at closely or examine, but, due to its metaphorical travels, it also carries the meaning now of a mental outlook or view (*American Heritage Dictionary*). It is worth noting that the early connection of vision and light would have lent *perspective* a metaphysical meaning of divine truth and knowledge from ancient times to the Enlightenment (see Guillén 287). After Milton and seventeenth-century philosophy and literature, though, a growing secularization through the eighteenth and nineteenth centuries altered this connection. For Descartes, for instance, vision and light were associated with human reason, not a divine eye.

Following Erwin Panofsky's *Perspective and Symbolic Form* (1927), an argument based in Cassirer's theory of "symbolic forms," it has been customary to associate linear perspective with the Renaissance, the period Panofsky privileged as developing the concept. Panofsky's narrative of the origin of perspective is a modern, retrospective construction which has had enormous influence on the discipline of art history, but has not gone unchallenged. Art historians note that perspective was not understood as such in the Renaissance, nor was perspective practiced as a single technique, nor was space as a concept familiar to Renaissance artists in the same way it is to us (see Guillén; Melville 1990; Elkins 1994, 8; and Mirzoeff 1999, 38, 51).

The codification and historization of the perspective paradigm and representational realism, then, has a vexed and complicated history. Moreover, it is a history that spans several disciplines, not only art history but philosophy, literature, literary criticism, and literary theory. While it cannot be the purpose of this book to untangle all the knots of this history, or even to mention them all, still, the stakes of this project cannot be fully understood without a brief historical account of the literal and metaphorical dimensions of this crucial concept.

Important steps were taken towards a theory of single-point linear perspective prior to the Renaissance, for example by the Greeks and Romans, who deployed a sense of depth in their architecture and by Abu Ali Hasan Ibn al-Haitham or Alhazen (965–1039), known as the father of modern optics, an Islamic mathematician who studied vision, physics, and geometry. Yet classic or linear perspective did not become formalized until the fifteenth century in Italy. Usually Brunelleschi is mentioned as the first person to understand, through mathematical principles, that parallel lines in a plane appear to meet, as they extend further from the viewer, along a horizon line where they vanish. Brunelleschi also understood scale—that the size of visible objects decreases the farther away they are from the viewer. Other artists famous for employing perspective included Masaccio, Ghiberti, and Ucello.

Using such rules of perspective helped painters gauge the size of objects in relationship to the eye and to distance. It was left to Leon Battista Alberti to codify the rules of perspective for artists in *De Pictura* (1435), in which he introduced the image of the window frame, and for the literate public in his vernacular text of the following year, dedicated to Brunelleschi: *Della Pittura*. Single-point perspective was not the only perspective used; for example, multiple vanishing points, anamorphosis, and aerial perspective were also employed. When I speak of linear or classical perspective, I am referring to a single fixed monological, mechanical viewpoint of a stable observer perceiving a world outside of the self in terms of a geometric grid with a single vanishing point. This method was used by artists to create a picture resembling reality, as if the eye mirrored the reality outside it.

PERSPECTIVE, DESCARTES, PANOFSKY, AND THE AFTERMATH

Scholars have often characterized Western modernity from the Renaissance to the nineteenth century as dominated by the visual, not only because of the hold of the perspective paradigm in art, but also because of the rationalization of seeing in the philosophy of René Descartes (*Discourse on Method* 1637). Yet how did perspective become linked with subjectivity, thus solidifying its massive influence through what Martin Jay has termed Cartesian perspectivalism?

Decartes humanized perspective. He viewed light as an emanation from an object, thus separating light from its metaphysical, metaphorical connection to the divine. In explaining vision, he used common examples, such as that of the blind man, to illustrate his theories about the senses. Even more importantly, as a rationalist, he located perception in the human brain, not the eye, even incorporating Kepler's new ideas about inversion of the image on the retina into part of the relay process that must exist, he felt, from eye to brain. The brain is the location of judgment: "perception, or the action by which we perceive," he maintains, "is not a vision . . . but is solely an inspection by the mind" (Descartes 63). For Descartes, then, the mind registers, processes, and judges the truth and accuracy of what the eye absorbs. Though sometimes misread, perspective for him was thus a mathematical law, based in geometry and the idea of resemblance to reality, but it also, at the same time, was a figuration rather than a faithful mirroring of reality.

Descartes's ideas about seeing and knowing are usually unhelpfully compressed with elements of Renaissance linear perspective, so that perspectivalism has come to stand for rationalism and his quest for epistemological certainty. In this compression, critics put aside the fact that Descartes's theory of vision was founded in skeptical doubt about the senses' certain apprehension of the world. Yet there are obvious connections between the perspectival paradigm and Descartes.

For example, Panofsky himself argues that Renaissance perspective anticipates the work of Descartes, because it inaugurates a mode of thinking about the relationship of subject to object, of mind to thing. Arguing that forms of spatial organization in artworks, of any era, correlate with and influence modes of perception of the ages in which they are produced and received, Panofsky sees perspective as far more than a geometrical schema. He maintains that perspective is a technique and a metaphor for a worldview, that which connects the psychological, cognitive, social, cosmological, and scientific/mathematical practices of a geographical and cultural moment. "For us," he argues, "perspective is quite precisely the capacity to represent a number of objects together with a part of the space around them in such a way that the conception of the material picture support is completely supplanted by the conception of a transparent plane through which we believe we are looking into an imaginary space" (77). Just as Descartes is uncertain about the eye and reality, Panofsky sees art as illusionistic.

While some interpreters of Panofsky have focused on the implications of his location of perspective in the Renaissance and challenged his notion of a worldview, and others have complicated his remarks about symbolic form, yet others have argued that Panofsky is more concerned with the self-reflexive qualities of art and the choices of a viewer than the mirroring qualities implied by the model. As Margaret Iverson puts it, for Panofsky, "Art is no longer regarded as a mimetic depiction of objects seen; rather it reflexively includes the acknowledgment that it is a highly formalized kind of performance aimed at a spectator" (4). In other words, on one level art is performative. It *does* something to someone.

Taking account of subjectivity, rather than implying all viewers are the same, Panofsky sets the stage for later interpretations of visual event "defined by the interaction between viewer and viewed" (Mirzoeff 1999, 13). Panofsky writes: "Perspective subjects the artistic phenomenon to stable and even mathematically exact rules but on the other hand, makes that phenomenon contingent upon human beings, indeed upon the individual: for these rules refer to the psychological and physical conditions of the visual impression, and the way they take effect is determined by the freely chosen position of a subjective 'point of view'" (67).

Too often, in my view, Cartesian perspectivalism has become a collapsed and overgeneralized concept. Critics have buried Descartes's doubts about the senses and have similarly slighted Panofsky's relevant insights into performativity and subjectivity.[5] Grootenboer is right in her assessment: "I think perspective has shaped an image of our visual field that we assume must be correct when we find proof of it in painting and in photography. Hence perspective has provided us with a model of looking and, consequently, with a mode of interpretation, whose consequences we, unlike Kepler, do not quickly recognize" (119). Too often taken as a method of mimetic resemblance and copy, rather than as a self-reflexive representation addressed to a spectator, perspectivalism was easily reduced in complexity and corralled into binarized explanations.

Drawing out some of the complications, Mieke Bal argues that the Cartesian cogito sustaining objective epistemology is itself a mini-narrative in first person. "Perspective elides the subject, already inscribed, in the viewpoint seen as the origin of subjectivity" (191). The entire conception of objective knowledge has to be contradictory (Bal 1996, 170–71). The structuralist Hubert Damisch would agree that perspective is characterized by the illusion of neutral objective third-person representation and that it works due to an identificatory effect premised on first person; he goes further to suggest that the subject of perspective, interpellated by a painting and interpellating a painting, "holds by a thread" and is not stable or fixed. He convincingly shows how the classical perspective paradigm is a "formal apparatus like a sentence" (446). Ultimately it can inform perception or orient it, but there is more power in polymorphic perception itself and in what paintings do to a spectator than in what they represent or the paradigm itself.

NINETEENTH-CENTURY ART AND LITERATURE

Theorists in cultural studies, film studies, and art history long supported a single narrative of a hegemonic Cartesian perspectivalism that begins to break down in the nineteenth century (see Crary 1992; Jenks 1995). As is well known, some, notably Crary, have asserted that a new kind of visuality was born in this period that grounded truth in the human body and processes of perception. In his highly influential *Techniques of the Observer*, Crary explains how specific optical instruments, practices, and institutions of the nineteenth century (stereoscope, kaleidoscope, diorama, panorama, and others) shape both the viewed and the spectator, defining what can be seen and how it can be seen. When optical instruments became sites for power and knowledge, Crary contends, following Foucault, a new form of visuality became dominant. Still, since he recognizes that the history of the observer is "not reducible to changing technical and mechanical practices any more than to the changing forms of artworks and visual representations" (8), he rightly maintains that "art and science were part of an interlocking field of knowledge or practice" (9).

Many critics working within nineteenth-century studies have usefully adapted and corrected some of Crary's research, particularly in light of the increased speed of time and space and the transience of everyday life in the nineteenth century (see critics on tourism, such as Schievelbusch; on urban aesthetics, Vadillo; and for a corrective reading regarding poetry, see Groth). Others have taken a further look at the impact on the culture of realism of new optical technologies and mass visuality (Friedberg 1993), while still acknowledging that a nineteenth-century viewer is constructed through many social forms. Such critics have generally agreed that an observer specific to the nineteenth century exists not as a transcendental subject but as an effect of a force field of discursive relations and amidst varied "reality effects."

Still, as some art historians and literary historians have pointed out, there are aspects to Crary's argument and method that do not persuade entirely. For instance, how is it possible that visual technologies, varied as they were and dependent on various aspects of perception, disciplined both the observer and the visual field (Mitchell 1994; I. Armstrong 2008)? It is important that Crary emphasizes the domination inscribed in modes of vision. Yet Crary's Foucaudian model of discourse/counter-discourse leads him to overlook practices of vision or kinds of observers or looks that might be multiple. Mirzoeff thus offers a valuable corrective when he suggests that "visual culture is always contested and that no one way of seeing is ever wholly accepted in a particular historical moment" (1999, 44).

An art historian who is eager to overturn the 'rupture' narrative about Modernism, and place change seventy-five years earlier, Crary still offers no analyses of what different art forms were doing at a time when the pictorial was dominant across genres. Though he demands a rethinking of realism, he avoids privileging art forms as a major influence on consciousness, precisely because this strategy has been followed, he says, too often. Nor does he apparently agree with J. Hillis Miller in judging nineteenth-century art to be *about* consciousness.

Despite his laudable focus on the early nineteenth-century in England, Crary's neglect of key Romantic and Victorian constructs, in his account of the waning of the perspective paradigm, is hardly unique. Eminent visual studies critics such as Nicholas Mirzoeff and Martin Jay join theorists from Erich Auerbach to philosophers such as Maurice Merleau-Ponty and numerous others in repeatedly bypassing the bulk of the nineteenth century to cite Impressionism and Modernism as the end point of classical perspective's hegemony in the visual and verbal arts.[6] One group of art historians places the end even later, when they cite Post-Impressionism and the split of illusionistic painting into component parts as the end of perspectivalism in art. Occasionally, literary critics mention Henry James as a precursor to impressionistic techniques, as we find in Virginia Woolf, because of his explorations of point of view, interior monologue, consciousness, and perception.[7]

However, it is critical to rethink the art works of the early to mid-nineteenth century across a range of genres, precisely to intervene in histories of the visual which persist in skipping to modernism, despite arguments against an historical model of rupture. For instance, when Nicholas Mirzoeff mentions examples of montage in the 1920s and 1930s as revolutionary, because they extend skepticism to realistic images, he seems entirely unaware of the print history and combination photographic art and editing rooms of the Victorian period. Yet combination photographs in the mid-nineteenth century, as we will see, while aiming to create whole views of reality, betray joins and unstable perspectives that serve to undermine the real, as much as they may mirror it.

In a talk/essay from 2005, Crary refers back to his decision to proceed in *Techniques of the Observer* without featuring artworks. Here he takes up several paintings "as primary pieces of evidence" that problematize the relationship between spectator and image (Crary 2008, 59). "There is a general epistemological inconclusiveness in which perceptual experience had lost the primal guarantees that once upheld its privileged relation to the foundation of knowledge," an uncertainty he accounts for by external factors (such as developments in lamp light) and an increase in subjectivism (60–61). In the pictures Crary selects, the objects have unstable features. In thematizing the images, Crary reduces the force of his argument. We need a formal analysis of kinds of engagement with vision and knowing, within image and text, with a detailed study of form for what it does to a spectator.

In my view, nineteenth-century art does not offer an epistemic rupture, in the sense of something radically new, but a continuation of the perspective paradigm with a quest for mastery and identification, but also with its uncertainty and performativity foregrounded. At the same time, nineteenth-century art experiments with new visual paradigms. Not enough work has yet been done in point of view or perspective. For instance, our understanding of realism in the Victorian novel, in particular of modes of narration, is still in the beginning stages. Perhaps Jonathan Culler's recent call to toss out the concept of *omniscience* is worth further investigation. Moreover, it was not the novel form, but poetry, that saw the most radical transformation of mimetic conventions in literature through its radical reconfiguration of lyric expression by a hybridic relationship to drama. In all nineteenth-century innovation in form, fictional or poetic, a greater burden for meaning is placed onto the spectator, the you, as the "I/eye" and as the connection of light to divinity diminishes in authority.

As is well known, Cartesian perspectivalism was critiqued by twentieth-century theorists for its claims to objective reason and unmediated truth by a dispassionate, monocular observer. As part of this investigation, theorists have proposed other visual regimes than that of the mastering, male-gendered, disciplining perspectival *gaze*. For instance, art historians have proposed the *glance* (Bryson), a quick, mobile, sideways look at surfaces. Gender critics as well have been especially influential in rethinking and undermining the gaze they have targeted as masculine and straight (see Mulvey; Doane; Irigaray; Fuss). Critics of culture and of film took up Walter Benjamin's urban stroller (1935) in positing a flâneur and a flâneuse, a mobile viewer, unrestrained rather than fixed (Nord; Friedberg 1993). Moreover, numerous historians of tourism, display, spectacle, and travelogue have stressed that vision is not only historically but also geographically shaped. It matters where one is as to how one sees and to how one looks. Yet despite these advances, it strikes me that few critics have paid attention to the generic range and media-rich heterogeneous regime of vision that enlists divergent observers in the nineteenth century. British artists developed innovative uses of light and space, experimented with ambient viewers and fixed views, fixed viewers and darting eyes, and encouraged oscillations among points of view, as they foregrouded self-reflexive negotiations of forms of mastery.

ON FORMS AND MEDIA

The goals for a book of this size must be modest, though my chapter range is ambitious. In the company of literary and cultural critics such as Isobel Armstrong and E. Warwick Slinn, I am committed to demonstrating the political importance of performative aesthetic forms. Many of the most interesting nineteenth-century texts, visual or verbal, are highly self-conscious about representation and, because directly concerned with hermeneutic problems, demanding of a reader-viewer. I wish to broaden such critical investigation across and between media. Because of the interaction between and among the arts during the nineteenth century and because artists often themselves worked in both literary and visual media, it is important to study the arts as part of a dynamic and changing cultural field rather than in isolation.[8] At the same time, we must retain the distinction that visual and verbal arts are not reducible one to the other.[9] While interesting in their own right, the visual and verbal examples I have chosen also allow me to show the period's wide range of experiment in England with monocular perspective. These texts enact cultural critique through dialogic and dialectic processes I will examine.[10]

The following chapters form a series of case studies. They are united by the fact that Victorians fully recognized that perspective was itself complex and multifaceted, never singular.[11] An inherited rigid use of Renaissance perspective was, for these artists, whether in painting, photography, or literature, not only reductive and false, but also unwanted as a curtailment of the visual and imaginative processes, mental sensations, and moral sentiments they wanted to retain.

Chapter 1 builds on the Introduction, with examples from J. M. W. Turner, William Dyce, and Romantic and Victorian poetry to show how in the early nineteenth century, both visual and verbal art challenged monocularism, often overtly and even with humor. In drawing attention to visual and verbal forms, I am less invested in content or thematics than in inquiries about formal experiment. The chapter concludes with an examination of William Morris's early essay on gothic seeing—recording his second visit to Amiens Cathedral—and his optically innovative poem "The Haystack in the Floods."

Chapter 2 examines the double art of Dante Gabriel Rossetti, in which painting and poetry are physically paired and a mobile reader viewer must go back and forth physically and mentally from text to painting in order to "see" and "know," but also to act. Rossetti's "double art" subtly but importantly alters the ideal of "unity" proposed in the eighteenth century between the sister arts. It is an extension of work started by William Blake in *Songs of Innocence,* where he eschews verbal/visual unity in favor of textual and pictorial commentaries on each other. Rossetti shares Blake's belief in what Northrup Frye first called "composite art"—the joining of distinctly different genres and of different reading and viewing experiences. Especially in his late works, Rossetti importantly attempts to blur differences between image and text at the same time that he solicits and constructs a mobile reader/viewer who must negotiate distance and difference. I wish to complicate our present understanding of Rossetti's double art and use it productively to open up questions about mobile and embodied seeing.

Chapter 3 explores the illusion of a recreation of reality prompted by the photograph, i.e., as a supposed mirroring of an object that surpasses other forms of mimesis. It concerns the theory and practice of Henry Peach Robinson. His professionally made combination photography, a form which tries to efface spatial disjunction among parts of the photograph, but which reveals gaps and stitches at the same time, raises important questions about who sees what and what is seen. The mirror and natural light photography of the amateur Lady Clementina Hawarden, on the other hand, explores spatial disjunctions that she connects to that time of life we now term adolescence. While photographs by Robinson and Hawarden may seem wholeheartedly to support classical perspective and its codes of realism, I will argue that Peach Robinson challenges mimesis through the joins of his photographs and through reference to gestural codes and intertextual references to paintings and poems. Hawarden does so, I maintain, through her manipulation of light, shadow, and doubling, inviting fractured, dual, and multiple perspectives.

Chapter 4 studies the challenges to omniscient narration and focalization in fictions of the 1860s, including Wilkie Collins's *The Woman in White* (1860) and George Eliot's *Silas Marner* (1861), as novelistic instances of the techniques of perspective explored brilliantly by Robert Browning in *Dramatic Lyrics* (1842) and in dramatic poems such as "Pippa Passes" (1841) and *The Ring and the Book* (1869). Browning's, Collins's, and Eliot's explorations of point of view also prefigured what such authors as Thomas Hardy in *Tess of the d'Urbervilles* (1891) would go on to do in complicating issues of objective truth in fiction and in revealing biased subjectivity at the heart of "third-person narrative," a supposedly "objective" presentation.[12]

A Coda encourages new directions for study across media and genres.

It is important to differentiate my interpretive assumptions from those of others. I do not see form as a literal or visual, conscious or unconscious *resolution* of historical and ideological contradictions or ruptures which the critic can then expose. This interpretive model about form and ideology remains too narrow in its implications about history, authors, texts, and readers, as well as too unquestioning of critical authority. To the contrary, nineteenth-century forms work not to paper over ideological contradictions but to call attention to them *as* papered over—as irresolvable and as raising questions about their very authority.

In other words, the artwork, not the contemporary critic, does the job of defamiliarization. The artwork, negotiating perspective, holds in solution contradictory perspectives and stages a dialogue which exposes the strengths and limits of perspective, while maintaining gaps for alternative points of view. And it compels a rethinking and reviewing on the part of the viewer and reader about (and these terms are not opposites or serially parallel): representation and experience, viewing and reading, affect and judgment.

Cultural critique is often associated with disidentification or with irony or parody in postmodernist theory. Because the ironic mode is often employed in nineteenth-century literature and visual arts, I want to make clear that the self-reflexive testing and questioning of mon-ocular perspective and Cartesian consciousness that I see in the verbal and visual representations I treat here does not always take the form of detachment as a basis for overturning of cultural norms. The process of questioning and testing, via perspectives and double forms, can regis-ter a nineteenth-century discomfort with any exclusive view. Still, this kind of art does not necessarily enact critique in the sense of judgment as much as it may explore points of view and expose the strengths and limits of each and place them for a reader or viewer side by side. Often it holds two simultaneous and contradictory attitudes in a tension, where one continually redefines and reopens the question of the other *or* where they exist as equally tenable because they exist within different systems of understanding and interpretation. Sometimes, as well, resistance to classical perspective simply registers a statement about objectivity or about consensual truth. It may point to a loss of a single truth, resistance to dogmatism, a quest for a redefined truth, acknowledgment of partial truths, or a re-understanding of the complexions and complexities of truth. In some cases, it may give up on truth.

CHAPTER ONE

Nineteenth-Century Challenges to Renaissance Perspective

Art is the secret of how to produce by a false thing the effect of a true.
—*Thomas Hardy on J. M. W. Turner, as quoted by Florence Hardy, 284*

HISTORICAL AND CRITICAL CONTEXTS

This book assumes as context the nineteenth century's well-documented interchanges among the sister arts and new technologies. Photographers "illustrated" poems; poets wrote about painters and paintings; painters drew heavily on literature for their subject matter and composed poems to be displayed with their paintings; prose writers incorporated new visual literacies into their thematics and form. As crucial components of a history of nineteenth-century visual and verbal literacies, the manifold interactions I examine here help to illuminate aesthetic theories and practices: dominant, emergent, and residual, currently being pieced together and rethought by cultural critics.[1]

During a time of increasing cultural debates about vision, realism, and the status of representation, artists across disciplines experimented freshly with optical clarity and obfuscation, and with double and multiple points of view, both within texts and between texts presented together. They questioned a stable relationship between subject and object and often resisted the era's growing scientific rationalism through composite art, combination printing, dramatic lyrics, mirror photography, multiply narrated or focalized novels, and montage.[2] By testing both visual and verbal boundaries, such formal innovations not only introduced new ways of beholding "reality" but also affected the way their beholders saw and knew themselves.

In short, the art forms I examine here placed new responsibilities on the observer-reader through self-reflexive modes of presentation. Sometimes exposed to a play of subjective and objective views in dialogic relation, this reader/viewer is, at other times, confronted with a confusion or fragmentation of views that similarly tests his interpretive capacities. The dramatic monologue and related forms, by way of example, especially those by Browning and Tennyson, challenge the Cartesian dualism of self and other (see Martin; I. Armstrong 1993; and Slinn 1991). Reconciliation, wholeness, and transcendence are replaced by a process of exchange in which one perspective is tested, altered, or replaced by another.

Such innovative forms are at odds with the epistemology of classic realism and push its boundaries. When Jennifer Green-Lewis notes that realism is an "ostensibly consensual mode of representation, since to objectify a world . . . requires a shared agreement, a complicity in what the object status of the world might be,"[3] her *ostensibly* carries much weight. The epistemology of classical perspective, stressing third-person omniscience and mastery, whether offered in painting, photography, or literature, is itself illusionary.[4] Classical perspective is not only troubled by subjective vision—rather than supplanted by it, as Jonathan Crary tends to argue in his genealogical argument—but it is also, in fact, intertwined with it in a relationship of hybridity. Each term is constitutive of the other rather than oppositional, but does not resolve to a third term.[5] It is this very unresolvable hybridity that is explored by the art forms of the period.

John Ruskin's writings on vision and perception, especially his formulation of the gothic, developed in *Modern Painters* (1843–60) and *The Stones of Venice* (1851–53), dramatically influenced the forms of his era's poetry and painting. Crucially, Ruskin's theory of the gothic validates a way of seeing, reading, and knowing that is based on gaps or inconsistencies, rather than grounded in notions of right perspective or unity and which was a shaping force in aesthetics, both visual and verbal.[6] This chapter takes up examples by Turner, Dyce, the dramatic monologue, and Morris as it builds a case inductively, across media and genres, for innovative nineteenth-century treatments of space and time, light, seeing, and multiple perspectives.

THE EXAMPLE OF J. M. W. TURNER

J. M. W. Turner, deeply schooled in art, music, and poetry of the eighteenth century, still often departed from tradition in his choice of content, handling of space, and uses of color as he sought to elevate landscape to the level of history painting. Moreover, his late art goes so far as to demand a new kind of viewer. From one of Turner's very first pencil and watercolors, *The Chancel and Crossing of Tintern Abbey, Looking towards the East Window* (1794), in which he reconfigures space and light and shrinks figures in size, we can see his departure from traditional drawing methods of both architecture and landscape. His 1829 *Ulysses Deriding Polyphemus—Homer's Odyssey,* exhibited at the Royal Academy in that year and in 1842, however, was rightly called by Ruskin "the central picture in Turner's career."[7] This makes it one of the most important paintings of the nineteenth century. The large (52 ¼ x 80 in. [132.5 x 203 cm]) scene, now in the National Gallery, London, was first sketched by Turner in the Wey, Guildford Sketchbook of 1807. In conception and exhibitions, it spans the major part of his career. Based on a section of Book IX from Homer's *Odyssey,* it pushes both the visual and verbal boundaries of a classical tradition of representation.

Although Turner bases his painting on a specific narrative moment in the *Odyssey,* he fits the classical myth of Ulysses into a larger interpretation of nature that goes far beyond any capturing of a classical antecedent. J. Hillis Miller has noted that "many of Turner's most celebrated paintings are illustrations of preexisting verbal documents,"[8] and, in this instance, art critic John Gage has stressed the painting's fidelity to Alexander Pope's translation.[9] Yet Turner's painting does not encourage the reading/viewing of a linear, teleological narrative. By the time he finished *Ulysses Deriding Polyphemus—Homer's Odyssey,* the painter had come to rely less on classical texts and forms. Through the many sea and sky pictures of his career to that point, he had frequently erased the vanishing point in light, as he does here, a technique he learned from Claude Lorrain. Yet he had also begun to develop the vortex as an organizational principle, which is evident in the handling of the clouds swirling around Polyphemus in this painting.

Although earlier passages of the *Odyssey* are presupposed in Turner's painting, Turner here mocks visual narratives that rely on a preexisting narrative, as well as linguistic meanings that rely on preconceived understandings. It is highly significant that Turner illustrates neither the attack on the Cyclops, nor Odysseus' taunting of the monster—saying "Nobody"—when the Cyclops asks who blinded him. Instead, Turner illustrates a later episode when Odysseus, having returned to his ship with his surviving men, and now sailing away, boastfully identifies himself by shouting out his real name to the giant, "Nobody didn't hurt you, Odysseus did!" In Turner's rendition, the sail states the Greek hero's name for anyone who can see it and read it, thus calling attention again to Polyphemus' limitations and calling upon the viewer to exercise sharp eyes. Odysseus' declaration of his identity provokes Polyphemus' father, the god Poseidon, to condemn the Greek mariner to a state of further wandering. Turner sets off this narrative moment of disastrous self-assertion into a purposely grand panorama of ships, figures, and natural phenomena, where the giant, enveloped in dark clouds, can barely be seen, and the relatively small figure of Odysseus faces away from the viewer towards the dawn and exit passage he is about to take in the distance.

Turner's scene thus ironizes the very moment of the epic hero's revelation of identity. Odysseus, thinking he has power over Polyphemus and assuming that he has secured smooth sailing, overreaches himself. Moreover, apparently Odysseus does not see a giant rock (also looking like a cloud) that the monster has hurled towards his ship with a flip of his arm. The canvas plays up ironies about breakdowns in visual communication. There is a shade or retina over the eye of the dawning sun, as if to suggest that Polyphemus is not the only blinded "I/EYE" here. Odysseus too is metaphorically blinded by hubris and, consequently, diminished. Turner takes the great hero Odysseus and robes him in red, the color to which Turner says the eye moves first, only to mock him. Reducing Odysseus to a speck in the giant natural universe portrayed in the picture, as he has done in many prior pictures with figures, Turner makes him positively puny compared to the equally diminished Polyphemus. It is perhaps not too fanciful to think of Odysseus here as a modern "Where's Waldo?" figure, dressed in red and almost lost in a swirl of other colors and images; actual viewers in front of the painting must puzzle it out. Turner picks up on Homer's own ironizing of Odysseus and maximizes it, enveloping the hero in a huge scene of volcanic fury, sunrise, numerous mariners, other ships, rocks, a mountain, smoke, Turner-invented Nereids, and, as Ruskin put it in *Modern Painters* V, a sky "the colour of blood" (7.438n).

Yet Turner's irony is further layered. The painter's self-identification with Odysseus as the blinder of a monstrous monocularity attests to his self-conscious awareness of the power of a large universe in which he is but one voice. His lonely, artistic authority is compromised by overwhelming external conditions. On the other hand, he calls attention, all the more, to the odds against which he fights and the visual markers with which he asserts himself.[10]

Turner also reaches out to ironize the entire classical tradition—not only in literature but also in painting, not only in content, but also in form, not only in art, but also in nineteenth-century viewing and inter-preting of art. Blindness as metaphor also extends to the viewer. The blinded, one-eyed Polyphemus, whom Odysseus taunts, also acts as an equivalent of the thwarted expectations of all those Philistine consumers, Turner's eyeless public, who had misread his art. Ruskin himself picks up on this connection between the Cyclops and the audience when he chooses this key painting to bemoan Turner's public "destiny" (*Turner, The Works of Ruskin* 13: 136) to be underappreciated by "the one-eyed people" who derided the painter's early work.

Even in their responses to this painting, critics complained about being *victimized* by the intensity of colors and stagelike setting. The *Literary Gazette* of May 9, 1829 states: "Although the Grecian hero has just put out the eye of the furious Cyclops, that is really no reason why Mr. Turner should put out both the eyes of us, harmless critics. . . ."[11] Odysseus may deride Polyphemus, but *The Morning Herald* (5 May 1829) derided the painting as "a specimen of *colouring run mad*—positive ver-milion—positive indigo, and all the most glaring tints of green, yellow, and purple contend for mastery of the canvas, with all the vehement contrasts of a kaleidoscope or Persian carpet" (as quoted in *Turner 1775–1851*, 133; emphasis in original). The reactions are correct: Turner's colors do indeed blind or disorient the viewer, as do the multiple sources of light (sun, fire, reflections, gleaming Nereids), intense coloring, and vari-ous points of focus. Most critics other than Ruskin, though, were reluc-tant to accept that Turner creates questions about how to view, where to look, and what a viewer sees. As the *Herald* plaintively remarked, "mastery" was not easy for a contemporary viewer of this painting. Yet mastery of this type was not often Turner's aim—as an examination of Turner's art up to this date illustrates, in both watercolors and oils, finished and unfinished, he often exploits odd vantage points, relies on multiple sources of light, and floods vanishing points with light.

Stalwart defender of laws of perspective that he was, Ruskin also recognized when such rules needed to be broken. In praising the 1829 painting, he has it both ways. Ruskin coyly noted: "I think we may not unwarrantably inquire how our Professor supposed that *that* Cyclops could ever have got into *that* cave" (Ruskin, *Turner, The Works of Ruskin*, 13: 138; emphasis in original). Ruskin implicitly linked Turner's work to that of the Pre-Raphaelites he had defended in public; they too had been excoriated for violating "perspective law." As Ruskin publicized them, both Turner and the Pre-Raphaelite newcomers were aiming at a different kind of vision.

If *Ulysses Deriding Polyphemus—Homer's Odyssey* is, in so many ways, a watershed turning point of J. M. W. Turner's career and predicts trends yet to come, his pendant paintings *Shade and Darkness—The Evening Before the Deluge* and *Light and Colour (Goethe's Theory)—The Morning After the Deluge—Moses Writing the Book of Genesis*, presented to the public in 1843 at the Royal Academy, even more explicitly defied classical perspective and narrative (for *Light and Colour*, see the cover). As pendants, they nullify a single point of view by establishing a dialectical relationship and calling on interpretive methods which read them in relation to each other. Even more, they mark dramatically the mounting change in styles of representation that over years had taken place in visual and verbal arts, on the edge of the dominant forms, from Blake onwards.

The impact of a shift from single, geometric, Renaissance perspective and classical subjects to nonrepresentational forms, bordering here on the abstract, would have far-reaching effects, cross-culturally in Europe as well as affecting other media in Britain. An historically provocative and theoretically exemplary instance of innovation, Turner's late career experiments with darkness, light, color, depth, and line, as evident in this pair of celebrated paintings, represent not only a revaluation of color theory but also a change in understandings of vision (see Douma).

Art historians argue that the fusion of the eye of the viewer with the circular moon and sun in these paintings marks a shift, within art, in conceptions about reality—from that which is external and passively received by the eye to that which the viewer creates. Perhaps this is nowhere more obvious than in animal forms represented in *The Evening Before the Deluge*, forms made far more abstract than in Turner's prior (rejected) painting on the same subject. From one angle, animal heads look like alligators, from another angle like horses. The viewer half-creates the forms depending on the angle from which viewing occurs. One moves back and forth in front of the painting to figure out what is actually being represented, as representational forms slide into each other.

Turner's color theory and its relationship to Goethe's *Zür Farbenlehre*, on the study or science of color, translated into English by Turner's friend Sir Charles Eastlake and referenced in the title of the second painting, animates this pair of quasi-Biblical paintings.[12] As the sun sets in *The Evening Before the Deluge*, the spectrum of colors moves through Goethe's negative colors of green, purple, and blue; with the sun fully risen in *The Morning After the Deluge* the colors are positive—red, yellow, orange. Yet as critics have noted, by mixing and blending his colors, Turner challenges Goethe's theory, which stresses the reading of colors as if they were signs. Rather, Turner believes that all color comes from light. Turner's art aligns pigments of color that can result in an "optical fusion," or a trick of the eye which makes a new color.

In other words, instead of representing nature, Turner tries, following Blake, to substitute an optical effect for the light and colors of nature. He creates paintings which invite the eye not only to behold but to *create* color and *imitate* light. Notably, contemporaries who visited his gallery at home compared his watercolors and oils to opals for their continuous play of blue, green, and red. Just as his Moses stands in the sun and the "I/eye" of God, so does Turner now place the viewer in a prophet-like position that allows not a godlike mastery of a view, but its co-creation. In an ironic rewriting of Genesis, Turner positions the viewer as the co-creator of the book documenting God's creation of the world. It is significant that Turner's pendant paintings were exhibited in the same year as the publication of volume I of John Ruskin's highly influential *Modern Painters*—a book that would go on, in a subsequent volume, to defend the painter from his persistent critics, precisely because, for the approving Ruskin, the artist had passed through a stage of realistic representation and moved well beyond it.

Yet we also need to note that, by choosing to paint the deluge and its aftermath as pendants, Turner also moved beyond his 1829 painting of the *Odyssey* to assert a Hebraic over a Hellenistic mode of representation. Here he collapses time and space realms in his evocation of beginnings: the destruction of history in the Noahitic flood, the creation told in Genesis, the writing of the Torah by Moses at Mount Sinai, and, with the signs of serpent and of the shepherd's crook, the crucifixion of and redemption by Jesus Christ.

By juxtaposing and blending time and space realms, Turner now questions linear perspective—verbal and visual perspective—even more radically than in his ironic rendering of Ulysses and Polyphemus when he blinds monocularity. In *The Morning After*, Moses is the sun in God's eye/I. He sits in the sun or on top of a sun-bathed Mount Sinai, in total radiance, with stylus writing the Torah/Old Testament. Turner refashions visually the history of painting, perspective, creation, and narrative by enabling the viewer to look at Moses in God's dazzling brightness with the stylus that will/did/does inaugurate a new order, as Moses and the viewer become the amanuensis-seer of the Divine.

Evoking the imagination of John Milton in *Paradise Lost*, Turner presents both a realm that is a "darkness visible" (I.62) and a "pendant world" (II.1052), hanging like an earring from a heaven of pure light. As an illustrator and an avid reader of Milton's epic, Turner wants us to remember that Milton was blind, like the prior great epic poet Homer, whose ironies he had adopted for his own purposes in the Polyphemus painting. Milton had claimed that, as epic writer, he would exceed Homer by becoming a second Moses, an inspired interpreter of a light unseen by the eyeballs of normal men and women. Turner's pendant paintings evoke precisely such a visual rendition of Miltonic imagination, what Samuel Taylor Coleridge had called in his 1817 *Biographia Literaria* the creative emulation of the *infinite I AM* (304).

Turner's painting, then, can be aligned with the verbal experimentations of a Romantic poetry that had steadily dramatized the interchange between a subject and an object. Literary Romanticism, too, I would argue, is a departure in ways of conceptualizing subject and object, not the source of or equivalent to that cultural shift.[13] Whether reacting to another human being or to nature or to a mythic figure or even to an art object, the Romantic poets conferred relevance on these others and obtained relevance from them in both one-way and reciprocal exchanges. William Wordsworth's poetry establishes a new relationship between subject and object in the history of poetry. He characteristically takes an "I" (or a Traveler or a Poet) and shows a subject/object relation that he then transforms so that the subject loses itself into the object but does not abandon reflective consciousness that allows for recollection.

Thus Wordworth's poems dramatize the processes of the human mind in relation to that outside the self. Samuel Taylor Coleridge in chapter 15 of *Biographia Literaria,* where he discusses Shakespeare and Milton, explains two types of union of subject and object that can be found in mixture, usually with one dominant, in all Romantic poetry. Shakespeare, he argues, is a protean subject/"I" who passes into all forms of character and passion in a chameleonlike fashion; Milton, he suggests, is an egotistical subject/"I" that attracts all forms and things to himself. In contrast, Romantic poetry also is a poetry about otherness, a Presence, a Being, God, gods, or a universal Mind or Unity. The realm of mystery is central because it means that Romantic poetry, for all its doubt, is grounded in a world of belief.

For their nineteenth-century successors in all media, however, this type of dynamic interaction of subject and object, in a context of belief and doubt, became more difficult, as did reliance on an authoritative and uncompromised lyric sensibility. The fortunes of the lyric "I" and its influence altered. The forceful shaping "I" of Wordsworth, which had itself become somewhat more tentative in poems such as "Elegiac Stanzas Suggested by a Picture of Peele Castle" (1805) and "The Excursion" (1814), would become, in the work of successors such as Shelley and Keats, Browning and Tennyson, even more elusive and eliding.

WILLIAM DYCE AND THE DRAMATIC MONOLOGUE

The dramatic monologue, a genre invented by the Victorians out of the Romantic conversation poem, dramatizes lyric expressivity by placing it into narrative or historical context. This plot against the lyric "I"—its authority and context—may be said to be true of many art forms in the period.[14] Put another way, much Victorian poetry follows the dramatic monologue in that it "demystifies the relationship between subject and object, and does not assume a primal unity on the part of the perceiving mind."[15] If the Romantic poets had celebrated and studied fusions and separations between subject and object, the Victorians confronted an inherited reality in which relations became even more difficult, not just relations between human beings, but relations to God and to a meaningful universe in which every creature, every "I," had a (formerly) special place. A painting such as *Pegwell Bay—Recollection of October 5, 1858* by the Scottish artist William Dyce illustrates the reach of this new precariousness felt by many, not only artists or writers. What is more, it offers reasons for that new sense of precariousness.

In the painting of a popular seaside resort in Kent, a dozen human figures are scattered throughout the painting in an arrangement dominated by the cliffs. Four appear in the foreground: a child stares to the left bottom foreground outside of the frame, not engaging with the viewer, but seemingly struck by some sight parallel to or behind the viewer. Two women look down for seashells, or fossils, or perhaps for oysters.[16] A third on the extreme right looks towards the viewer from beyond the midpoint. Engagement between figures and viewer is not established, but, in fact, refused. In the distance there are more figures, mostly male. To the right there is a single figure, referred to by the Tate commentary online as an artist (this figure is, by the way, often cut off or sliced in half in online reproductions).[17] Men in a group with donkeys to the right of midpoint testify to the mode of transport then popular for coastal tourism. But the position of all the figures is helter-skelter, arbitrary, as if they had all been caught momentarily on varying walks in different directions. None interact with others. Color and light are essential in this painting; the mood struck by the use of browns and yellows is half sickly, even nightmarish, and, at the same time, reminiscent of sepia photography. The humans' aloneness is given meaning by the very cliffs that dwarf them. For the rocks expose geological strata of calcified creatures who lived millions of years before in waters and pools such as the ones through which these later creatures, now dressed in nineteenth-century garb, are wading. The humans are mere objects here, puppets on a seashore, like that described by Matthew Arnold in "Dover Beach," during a time when the new science was questioning theocentrism and the timetable of Genesis. The 'objective' view offered by science could not only contextualize, but could also obliterate the importance of any individual perspective.

The sense of human puniness, captured by Dyce, is magnified by another element in the painting besides the spatialization of time handled through the cliffs. The day memorialized, October 5, 1858, was when Donati's comet streaked through the sky at its brightest. It is in the painting on its fall—but barely seen above the clouds on the horizon. The fact that it is nearly invisible reinforces the painting's emphasis, an emphasis markedly different even from the cosmic drama we have seen in a Turner painting. No longer do meteors or comets come to humans as warnings from the gods. This comet is as indifferent to the human shell collectors as they are to each other and to it. Only the artist figure might be said to notice it. Moving at a speed exceeding the figures, they now seem in slow motion, groping, preparing to be fossils themselves, when scaled against the vastness of sidereal space and geological time. The relationship of subject and object set up by Dyce's painting is but one mark of a dramatic change from a pre-Revolutionary, eighteenth-century mindset to Victorian sensibilities, a change that is psychological, cultural, social, scientific, and aesthetic. Dyce asks the viewer to take in the whole scene, to register kinds of change more fully and deeply than as just a holiday observer of husks of being, and to accept the coexistence of differing and irreconcilable perspectives.

In contrast to Turner's sky/sea/ship drama that diminishes Homer's epic hero and his monstrous other, the ironies offered by Dyce's vision of a comet against cliffs and shallow waters are more subtle and more far-reaching. Not only is the hero a Nobody as in Turner, but nobody, in the Dyce, is remotely heroic. Nothing is at stake but sea creatures and shells. No divinity is present, ancient or modern. The most significant and unusual event, Donati's comet, goes barely noticed. While a sole figure we take to be an artist figure looks up at the sky, there is no Moses to interpret or make meaning of this cosmic event. The sickly color of a yellow nightmare rather than golden sunlight stays with the viewer of the painting, as it asks: is your face down, too, or do you take notice of the comet? Is there anything to be made of it?

In Victorian poems the terms of self and other prove unstable. Problems of agency, consciousness, power, labor, and representation are foregrounded.[18] By way of brief example, "Tithonus," a special form of dramatic monologue called mask lyric, by Alfred Tennyson, sets into relief and even parodies the traffic between subject and object.[19] In addition "Tithonus," like the Dyce painting, foregrounds the loss of external, reliable sources of authority by featuring a goddess, but one we aren't even sure is listening, much less related in any other way to the "I," despite his calls and protestations.

Certainly if there is a relationship, it is a profoundly disappointed and negative one. The self mentioned in line 5 is an object, not a subject: "Me only cruel immortality / consumes" establishes the speaker as devoured, eternally, by an implacable universal authority. Yet the clause following in juxtaposition, "I wither slowly in thine arms," defines this same self in terms of a more subjective and intimate—and killing—relationship. The split and sliding of I/Me is already prepared for in the first line aurally with a mournful "Ay me. Ay me" retained from the original 1833 poem "Tithon" until the 1864 version of "Tithonus." The sound Ay recalls "I" and is yet just a sound, even as Tithonus is just a voice doomed to mourning a formerly whole self defined in terms of youth and masculine vigor.

When Arthur Hallam reviewed Tennyson's poems, he noted that his friend was writing a new "species of poetry, a graft of the lyric on the dramatic, and Mr. Tennyson deserves the laurel of an inventor, an enlarger of our modes of knowledge and power."[20] In "Tithonus," for instance, a poem perhaps surprisingly 'typical' of many others, two concurrent poems exist with the same words: a lyric expression and that lyric expression as an object of critique, when read as drama. The distance injected into the mask lyric and the related form of the dramatic monologue create a gap for critique of the speaker as not only subject but also object of the gaze and knowledge of a reader. This gap signals a plot against the lyric voice or pure expressivity, making it dependent on and answerable to larger forces, whether of history, society, contingency, or fate.

WILLIAM MORRIS AT AMIENS CATHEDRAL AND "THE HAYSTACK IN THE FLOODS"

While D. G. Rossetti, whom I take up in some detail in the next chapter, was perhaps the greatest immediate disciple of Ruskin, William Morris's early poems and prose pieces prove dramatically shaped by Ruskin's theory of the gothic. At twenty-four, Morris published one of the most original poetry books of the middle decades of the century: *The Defence of Guenevere, and Other Poems* (1858). His intimacy with the poetry of John Keats and Alfred Tennyson, with Sir Walter Scott's fiction, and with the paintings of D. G. Rossetti, augmented by his readings in Sir Thomas Malory, Jean Froissart, and Geoffrey Chaucer, might have led him to compose imitative poems, replete with the mystery, beauty, and heroism he associated with the Middle Ages. Moreover, Scott's novels, Ruskin's *Modern Painters* (1843–60), and Thomas Carlyle's *Past and Present* (1843), politicizing the aesthetic, had already established the Middle Ages as an historical foil and analogue for the moral and sociopolitical questions raised by an age marked by industrial capitalism and consumption. But the novelty of Morris's poetic experiments derived from other, additional sources. His own immersion in the gothic aesthetic from the age of eight, his apprenticeship with the architect G. E. Street in 1856 (the greatest Gothic revivalist of his day), and his fascination with the dramatic monologues of Robert Browning honed his ability to write poems that were simultaneously edgy, optically adventurous, and individualistic.

Morris's childhood had been filled with the reading of romances; his boyhood days at Woodford Hall were immersed in the rituals of an earlier England; his college days were spent among Oxford's spires and medieval, winding ways. Yet it was John Ruskin's definition of gothic that galvanized his already intense response to the Middle Ages. Even towards the end of his career, his interest in Ruskin's "The Nature of Gothic" did not wane; he printed it at the Kelmscott Press in 1892. Morris's own youthful essay on Amiens Cathedral, published a mere three years before his first volume of poems, helps to illuminate the Ruskinian underpinnings of "The Haystack in the Floods," a poem I shall subsequently discuss.

Walking in the literal footsteps of Ruskin in northern France, Morris considers the great Gothic cathedral of Amiens as a Bible to be read. Seeing Gothic face to face (in person and in its vast materiality) allows Morris to train the eyes of his readers to see the stonework come alive in a new way. Ruskin had upheld the social democracy of a community of medieval stoneworkers; Morris, however, entirely collapses the temporal past and present by leading us to "see." The proper optical attentions would, insists Morris, make the builders themselves live again through a community of Victorian spectators. As with art by Turner or Dyce or with the secrets of public, private, and performative in a dramatic monologue, however, what we could *not* see or know also mattered to Morris. Failures of vision or objects murky or masked were as important for Morris as what could be seen clearly. His was the eye of multiple vantage points, but not a totalizing vision.

Morris wrote "The Churches of North France: Shadows of Amiens" (1855) in his co-founded *The Oxford and Cambridge Magazine* as the first of a series. In the essay he duplicates in form that which he advocates in content: a blending of past and present perspectives in one time and space. Although Morris records the impressions of his second visit to Amiens, he writes at a meeting point of the horizons of past and present: as if seeing the architectural masterpiece for the first time. Longing prompts Morris, he confesses, to return to Amiens and to the other Gothic churches of Normandy. He tells us "how much I loved them" (289). At his second visit, he exults, the wonder for him at the cathedral's grandeur was still fresh: "I think I felt inclined to shout," he records, "when I first entered Amiens Cathedral" (293).

If the gothic, according to Ruskin, is to shock us into new ways of seeing in a metaphorical and a social as well as a literal sense, what new vista does Morris's essay on gothic wish to open? Morris, I argue, wants to reanimate the gothic itself, in its various permutations, in a sense to become it: its narrativizing, physicality, complexity, multiplicity, variety, appreciation of savagery, roughness, and disjunctions. Seeing gothic for Morris is an act of desire, founded on loss and lack. To effect a duplicate effect on the reader/viewer, Morris first invites us into a deep affectual relationship with him. Once in partnership, his "I" leads this reader's affective engagement with *him* to the Gothic cathedral *creators* revived through the Biblical narratives carved in stone through Old to New Testament and medieval figures and stories. In sum, he moves the reader/viewer from personal relationship to a community with past creators to an immersion into the stone creation itself, before bidding farewell to his cathedral.

Morris invites the reader/viewer to "see" by wandering in and out of the cathedral on a walk with him that educates us into the parts and details of Gothic style. Lindsay Smith is right to stress the various vantage points to which Morris refers, which make the essay less about the object of perception than about how and from where we see.[21] Yet "Shadows of Amiens" is also itself a shifting document—an invitation to mutuality in a church aisle, a memory piece, a self-reflexive commentary on memory and fact, a reflection on what we need to see or know in order to love, and a conclusion that resists language or full knowledge or full seeing.

In the essay's opening, the "I" and the "you" are separated. Morris's "I" is a guide who positions "you" to see—first as mounting to a town steeple or a house roof west of the cathedral (290). If "you" then looked up, he says, you would see the "mystery" of the rose window (291). The conditional becomes the present. From a lower position, in the "hot Place Royale here," "you can see nothing but the graceful spire" (291). Asking the reader, now as an intimate co-viewer, to look across, up, down, from far, from near, and from close up, Morris also anthropomorphizes the building—marking its ribs, crown, base, until he climaxes this description with the "mighty army of the buttresses, holding up the weight of the stone roof within with their strong arms forever" (292).

With the building a living thing, "I" and "You" can become a "We" in order to enter the cathedral together as if to be wed—moving first through the dimmed obscurity of shadow into a relatively well-lit and colorful interior and into a continuous present: "We go round under their shadows," says Morris, to "enter the church " and "we go down the nave" until at the transept "the stained glass in their huge windows burns out on us" (292–93). While Morris may be conducting a tour, he is also marrying the reader/viewer, moving inevitably and directly down the labyrinthine pavement towards the front of the cathedral into the canopied, carved stalls filled with sixteenth-century figures that come alive through jewel-like coloring.

Caught up in the narratives he sees depicted and those he recalls of Biblical stories witnessed on his first visit, Morris begins to share his memories of specific figures with phrases in mixed tenses and with mixed feelings: "I remember," "I do not remember in the least the order," "I remember too," "I wish I remembered," "I have dim recollection." While he can't recall all the details of each aspect, he delights in moving back and forth from a general to a specific view, from a normative to a difficult view, from the horizontal to the vertical view, from the wide to the narrow vantage point. "One can" even, he says "look down through a hole in the vaulting and see the people walking and praying on the pavement below, looking very small from that height and strangely foreshortened" (296). In telescoping or magnifying views, the viewer too becomes a speck or a panoramic eye caught in the imagined return view of that which it sees. Rather than considering the cathedral a geometric conception of space, Morris wants to know how a vast object like a cathedral is made visible, is visually processed and remembered, and, as a result, becomes known and thus felt.

As Morris moves among memory, desire, and present experience, the polychromatic appearance of the choir screen carvings and chapel tombs, lit by a vast nave and light from high windows, plunge him into a reverie of what the interior must have been like, a multifaceted jewel, when it was "painted from end to end with patterns of flowers & stars and histories" (296). He is intrigued by his own changing positions as a viewer, as well as by how light interacts with space and in the relationships of light to color to metaphor: "The sun was setting, when we were in the roof; and a beam of it, striking through the small window up in the gable fell in blood-red spots on the beams of the great dim roof" (297). Placing himself imaginatively in the cathedral before its large-scale whitewashing in 1771, he suggests erotically that he might have walked there from sunrise to sunset amidst a glow of color all around. Morris may not have known in 1855 that the cathedral's exterior western façade had also been decorated in multiple hues in the thirteenth century.[22]

Suddenly, Morris returns the reader/viewer to an easy chair, shifting register to comment on the essay he is writing. This section climaxes with the self-reflexive admission that this essay was not written at Amiens. Morris relies, he tells us, on photographs, as well as two sets of memories. Thus the "shadows" in the title of the essay are not only those within the cathedral, or a reference to its height dominance over other Normandy cathedrals, or a signifier for what we will never fathom, but literally refer to the dark bits of the photographs "where the shadows are deep," areas which "show simply nothing" (297). Despite impressions, memories, and photographs, some things are left unseen, unremembered, unknown, unprocessed.

Morris's reliance on contrary methods of capturing reality is in dialogue, with one revising the perceptions of the other (photographs capture details we may have forgotten; yet the eye captures color, the photograph does not; the eye gets a sweep of the whole, photographs do not; the eye absorbs impressions of grandeur which the photograph, "square-cut" and "brown" colored, does not). Photographs, while verifying facts or helpful in capturing general effects, may however even "dull" prior embodied impressions (298). Yet neither human perception nor mechanical aids can ultimately illuminate all the "shadows" of Amiens. Morris accepts the lack of a single centered subject or object, geographically, temporally, and experientially. He is not seeking to obtain a totality of perception or unity of object.

Before voicing his farewell to gothic seeing, Morris pauses at the Crucifixion scene to mention the inadequacy of language to capture the "loveliness of some of the figures carved here" (305). In particular a westernmost angel's female face draws him to emphasize the impossibility of words. "I am utterly at a loss how to describe it . . . I cannot say more about it." The text here foregrounds itself as writing, not authoritative voice, in what E. Warwick Slinn might refer to as "a discourse of self characterized by division and displacement, not harmony" (1991, 1). Like the dramatic monologue of the era, which challenges any easy opposition or knowledge of subject and object or self and other, the prose of gothic seeing ultimately asks the reader/viewer to entertain questions about vision, consciousness, and language. It is up to the reader to evaluate his relationship to both the seer and the seen.

In a final peroration, Morris's "I" and "eye" disappear into a description that does not locate itself authoritatively in either consciousness or vision. Rather, the I and eye blend into a final, magnificently accretive description. The speaker is both absent from our time frame—taking off, as it were, into all time frames—and yet present through a prevision. Suddenly, Amiens appears in all kinds of weather, August to February, warmed by heat and cooled by cold, bathed in colors and neutral tones and black, in moonlight and sunlight, until the very roses that one knows are carved begin to glow red, as if real, all the while remaining in a mystery of light and shadows.

Morris's poem "The Haystack in the Floods" (1858) pursues a similar distrust of words and engages in a similar experimentation with optical vision. Yet this poem carries that distrust and experimentation to a new level. Gaps between words now hold a physical and material dialogue on the page and contribute to broken, decapitated meaning. In other words, the poem, which concerns Jehane's prevision of her English lover Robert's beheading by his French foes, enacts that loss. It does so first by an overloading of sensual, closely packed, and layered words and images. Although the surface rhetoric of the poem seems to control a reading grounded in content, we must soon look beyond that level to other patterns, pictures, and textual repetitions in order to be shocked into the new perspective of gothic seeing.[23] Already at this early date, we find an adumbration of those techniques of structure and repetition that Morris would later perfect in the 1860s as an artist not of the window, but of the "wall and page" (see Helsinger 209).

From its *in medias res* start, the poem calls attention to itself as a construct, as a dense weaving of words, in order to rip familiar ground from the reader. It opens with two questions.

> Had she come all the way for this,
> To part at last without a kiss?
> Yea, had she borne the dirt and rain

> That her own eyes might see him slain
> Beside the haystack in the floods?

Are we being placed inside the ongoing present of a woman's interior monologue, or are we being guided by the indirect discourse of a third-person narrator who is commenting on a set of events after the fact? We don't know if the speaker addresses a question to herself or to us. We don't know if "Yea" answers the first question or serves as a bridge word setting up a parallelism between questions. Given the density of all poetry, we must therefore assume it is addressed to both and serves a dual function. Already, consciousnesses are mixed and confused. Only later in the poem will we understand this opening as a prevision; yet we still remain unclear about whether we are meant to regard it solely as a thought or as a thought reported as uttered and heard.

The fact that the central event concerns seeing the death of one's beloved is almost incidental at first to the problems faced by the reader—When? Who? What? A triple dislocation, of time, person, and event, is further reinforced by the fact that the reader must infer that the context is the Hundred Years War between France and England. Dislocation is intensified all the more by our sense that we exist in a mythic landscape as much as a real one.

The title of the poem, "The Haystack in the Floods," seems real enough. The title refers to a conical, darkened, yellow stack of hay in a flooded field. It is raining. In the middle of the events of the poem, Jehane will lie down and take a nap, "her head on a wet heap of hay" (120). Yet the word *Floods* and the shape of a conical haystack is disturbing. Though the reader's imagination might prefer to rest easy with a ritualized scene, something is awry. Alas, the presence of a flood should warn us at the start that this is not an ordinary scene or poem. The conical haystack sits in the flood, like a head in blood—a title and image, then, that carries shock and imaginative horror once one hears in rhymes and once one learns the events in the poem.

Morris is not interested in conceptualization. He expresses a situation of intense longing between lovers who reach out to each other in the horror of their separation through a dreamlike, visionary set of impressions. The haystack draws numerous meanings as a pregnant image. It stands for an agricultural period of history, for the rituals and routines of the natural world, for the vagaries of nature over which we have no control. Its singular, lonely object-like profile, in the middle of a landscape, recalling Robert's (or any lover's) severed head, calls up the darker side of medievalism—a near random violence that seemingly ruled the world (and Morris's nineteenth-century mythic view) of the Middle Ages. The poem is about this set of associations, and feelings attached to them, as much as it is "about" Jehane, Robert, or Godmar.

Morris reinforces a hypertextual sense of words serving as objects themselves by filling the poem with gaps after question marks, semi-colons, or exclamation marks (see lines 17, 19, 22, and 27, for example). The first gap is produced by the stanza separation after the first five lines, and before the next twenty-five, a gap which also cuts the rhyme by forcefully separating the octosyllabic half-rhyme of *floods/woods*. An equally deliberate use of literal spaces in caesurae creates a rising tension of separation, trauma, and loss. If the first gap separates her and he, "Far off from her; he had to ride" (17), the four gaps in these ten lines set up a pattern so that the eye traveling down, noting the first word after each gap, reads: *he /and/ she /yea*. This cluster works together in a countersong to join the very pronouns and people whom the poem will rend apart. A tension is constructed by words in the poem, therefore, which, on the one hand, separate the lovers and, on the other hand, subliminally, subconsciously, unite them again.

In addition to the countersong of a longing for union, there is a consistent prevision of destruction that occurs at the level of word and part of word. *Head* appears as part of a word or as a word in its own right numerous times before the beheading occurs at the level of poem content. Rain drips on her *head* (12); he rides a*head* (18); she weeps, made giddy in the *head* (24); they count thirty *head*s (38); in grief she tries to rend her coif from her *head* (42); she thinks her fore*head* bled (78) and turned her *head* away (79); Godmar's face turns red chin to *head* (82); he swears falsely by God's *head* (104); she falls asleep with her *head* on hay (120); at her 'no,' his *head* turns sharply round (126); Godmar bends back Robert's *head* (144); his men trample Robert's *head* to pieces (151); confronted with Godmar's promise he will have her drowned, she shook her *head* (156).

It may strike my reader as overkill to isolate such uses of one word. Yet Morris's artistry here is multiply tuned. He uses *head* as an object that is seen, imagined, felt, cut, and beaten. It is both agent and acted on, material object, location of reason, thing. In forcing the reader to see, hear, and read the word in various contexts, Morris sends the reader/ viewer into a previsionary mode, purposely dropping clues about the narrative he will not present clearly or straightforwardly. But he also increases the claustrophobia and hallucinatory quality of the poem and of the psyches represented, joining the reader to them, through such relentless repetition.

Morris writes an aural poem, as he tests the visual. It is also a poem longing for haptic perception and one of a forced reliance on eyesight. It is an exhausting poetry about being unable to effect change, even with prevision, in a world uncaring about what one feels, touches, sees, or knows. My brief analysis conveys, I hope, the brilliance of his radical testing of boundaries between reason and madness, truthful words and words that mask, and his refusal to treat either the subject or the object in traditional ways.

Like Jehane, the reader/viewer is asked to turn her head, to view the poem askance. Morris's protagonist exists in a previsionary stanza that deforms conventional reading and seeing skills. The stanza that heads the poem introduces a narrative that will, like Robert's head, be fragmented yet remembered.

CHAPTER TWO

D. G. Rossetti's Double Work of Art and the Viewer/Reader

Above all ideal personalities with which the poet must learn to identify himself, there is one supremely real which is the most imperative of all: namely the reader.
    —D. G. Rossetti, Doughty and Wahl[1]

Like Dante, he knows no region of spirit which shall not be sensuous also, or material.
    —Walter Pater, "Dante Gabriel Rossetti," 237

While at work on his first major painting, *The Girlhood of Mary Virgin*, in 1848 (figure 1), Dante Gabriel Rossetti composed a sonnet on the same subject. In March 1849, when the painting was shown at the unjuried Hyde Park Corner Free Exhibition, Rossetti saw it printed in the exhibition booklet and affixed it and a second sonnet on gold leaf paper to the frame.[2] The simultaneous presentation of reading and viewing materials on the general topic of Mary's girlhood required a mobile gaze and a dialectical engagement by a viewer/reader between two kinds of art. Previous Rossetti critics have noted that as part of their topic and goal, both his paintings and his sonnets offer multiple perspectives within them. This chapter will build on that work, arguing that by exhibiting paintings with poems attached, Rossetti exposes the viewer/reader to a series of shifting perspectives—literal and conceptual—which further undermine traditional mimesis and its accompanying epistemology.[3] Relying on an analytic understanding of how objects speak to and act on nonstationary viewer/readers, Rossetti explores a new relationship to the object being processed.

Figure 1. D. G. Rossetti, *The Girlhood of Mary Virgin*, 1848–49.
Oil on canvas, 83.2 x 65.4 cm. Tate Gallery, London

Rossetti's numerous incarnations of a relationship between poetry and painting started in the 1840s and reached their highest point during the 1870s and 1880s, when his paired sonnets and massive paintings of women, most often his beloved Jane Burden Morris or Alexa Wilding, achieved a complexity that greatly surpassed his earlier experiments. This chapter will examine two late pairs, *Astarte Syriaca* and *The Day-Dream*, against the earliest example of such pairings, *The Girlhood of Mary Virgin*, to see how Rossetti's double art evolved and what it can teach us about Victorian alternatives to traditional visual perspective and accompanying metaphysics and epistemology.

The Girlhood of Mary Virgin (1849), the first painting to feature "PRB" alongside a painter's signature, announces the Pre-Raphaelite movement as differing distinctively in subject, composition, and technique from paintings that had still supported the norms of unity, or the handling of content and perspective promoted by Sir Joshua Reynolds and the Royal Academy of Art. Previous critics have located this difference by stressing a pronounced dialectical rhythm which makes Rossetti's paintings and sonnets alike (see Fredeman; Stein; McGann, Rossetti Archive). They have noted that his destruction of traditional geometric perspective, his separation of content into sections reinforced by his use of color, and his choice of the sonnet form all force the viewer/reader to value parts, rather than hierarchizing sections into an integrated composition. Other Pre-Raphaelites, too, were known for their commitment to units and for differing ways of manipulating sharp detail.[4] As Chris Brooks aptly puts it, they practiced "a realism of parts, not wholes" (126).

Yet equally important is Rossetti's concurrent shaping of an ambient viewer/reader who must repeatedly negotiate two art forms that differ remarkably in size, in semiotic language, and in location. Rossetti physically undoes the traditional relationship of a single, stable exchange in space between viewer's eye and object. Even more to the point, within paintings and sonnets, Rossetti raises to consciousness struggle and translation among sign systems and interpretive methods. Materially, he forces the viewer/reader to move back and forth in space and in time between words and images.

The pairing of two art objects, requiring a complex dual response, was hardly new on the visual arts or literary scene. Companion pieces had long existed in the visual arts, literary, and sister arts traditions. In chapter 1, we have seen one example of Turner's pendant paintings: *Shade and Darkness—The Evening Before the Deluge* and *Light and Colour (Goethe's Theory)—The Morning After the Deluge—Moses Writing the Book of Genesis*. While this is not the place for a full genealogy of pendantry, it is worth recalling earlier pairs of drawings by William Hogarth, among other visual artists, precisely because of their vast influence and because of their social analytics. In poetry, examples as diverse as paired sonnets within Shakespeare's sonnet sequence or Milton's "L'Allegro" and "Il Penseroso" illustrate different uses and kinds of relationship.[5] In seeking the origins of pairing within literature, we probably have to go as far back as strophe/antistrophe, which was part of the three-part ode form in Greece (and thus part of every chorus in Greek tragedy) and to the rhetorical strategy of parallelism found in Plutarch's *Lives*.

Notably, such pendantry had become increasingly attractive to poets in the 1830s and 1840s as they continued self-consciously to explore problems of representation and alternatives to Romantic lyric subjectivity and as they drew upon other discourses such as social analysis and historical writing. In 1833 Robert Browning had published the dramatic monologues "Johannes Agricola" and "Porphyria's Lover" under the combined title "Madhouse Cells." In 1842 Tennyson, in dramatically revising poems from his 1832 volume, set up alternating views on the same topic. His changes to "The Lady of Shalott," for example, multiplied perspectives on a mythic story he had already exploited for issues of mirroring and point of view.[6] His own "Ulysses" and "Tithonus" would eventually be published, also, as a pair of alternating points of view, even as Browning would go on to explore dramatic lyric more fully in fifty poems of *Men and Women* (1855). Both Browning and Tennyson were engaged in experimentations of form as serving social and political agendas that required renovating, if differently, how we read and feel. Both exploited different ways of multiplying views, through poetic forms chosen (a series of juxtaposed monologues, dramatic monologue), through content (poems about point of view, transmission, or translation), through images and symbols (mirrors, the processes of art), and presentation method (pairing poems).

The most important recent predecessor for Rossetti, however, probably would have been William Blake's illuminated books, *Songs of Innocence* and *Songs of Experience,* not only because of the visual and verbal connection, but more precisely because Blake deploys composite visual and verbal elements with and against each other to shift a viewer/reader's perspective and understanding. Significantly, however, Rossetti does not make his visual and verbal art composite, like Blake's. Most often he accentuates a division or bar, or what McGann calls a gap, as he illustrates literally in his most famous painting, *The Blessed Damozel.* It is a bar he perceives between the material and spiritual worlds, and hence not only a separation between art forms. Although Rossetti seeks to transcend this separation, to imitate the medieval art which he admired for unifying the physical and the spiritual, he engages the separation as part of the message of his double art.

A viewer/reader seeing Rossetti's set of Marian materials displayed at the 1849 Free Exhibition would certainly have been exposed to just such a separation. He or she might have read the sonnets first and then turned his or her attention to the image, or could have read one sonnet in the exhibition booklet, looked at the painting, and only then have read the other sonnet.

Here are the two sonnets Rossetti invited viewers of *The Girlhood of Mary Virgin* to connect to the painting before them[7]:

This is that blessed Mary, pre-elect
    God's Virgin. Gone is a great while, and she
    Was young in Nazareth of Galilee.
Her kin she cherished with devout respect:
Her gifts were simpleness of intellect
    And supreme patience. From her mother's knee
    Faithful and hopeful; wise in charity;
Strong in grave peace; in duty circumspect

So held she through her girlhood; as it were
    An angel-watered lily, that near God
      Grows, and is quiet. Till one dawn, at home
She woke in her white bed, and had no fear
    At all, yet wept till sunshine, and felt awed;
      Because the fullness of the time was come.

These are the symbols. On that cloth of red
    I' the centre is the Tripoint: perfect each
    Except the second of its points, to teach
That Christ is not yet born. The books—whose head
Is golden Charity, as Paul hath said—
    Those virtues are wherein the soul is rich:
    Therefore on them the lily standeth, which
Is innocence, being interpreted.

The seven-thorn'd briar and the palm seven-leaved
    Are her great sorrow and her great reward.
      Until the end be full, the Holy One
Abides without. She soon shall have achieved
Her perfect purity: yea, God the Lord
    Shall soon vouchsafe His Son to be her Son.

Did the viewers, however, pause to read these two texts first? I suspect, instead, that the brilliantly colorful image, imitating an illuminated medieval manuscript in order to evoke the Middle Ages during Victorian times, would have initially captivated the majority of viewers, though we have no documented reception history.[8] In any case, the spectator would have had choices to make about seeing and reading. She or he would have consciously or unconsciously had to move back and forth among small units, both linguistic and pictorial, for a full experience of double art. Such movement is precisely what Rossetti sets up by choosing to pair and even condense two art 'languages.' While his first sonnet describes his topic, Mary, his second calls attention to cognition and vision, when he directs the reader to look: "These are the symbols. On that cloth of red" (1). The fact that Rossetti's directive sets out literally to move, involve, and educate a reader into becoming a viewer/reader is part of the very topic of the painting/sonnet set.

The painting compels attention, too, because, as several critics have noted, it doesn't present a traditional education scene for Mary, as we might see it handled in a medieval manuscript or by Giotto or later painters.[9] Rossetti offers something quite different with his new combination of sacred subject matter, intense color and handling, ordinary faces engaged in everyday activities, and disruption of traditional perspective.[10] In this regard, he lives up to Holman Hunt's expectations for the Brotherhood: "while artists must forever be beholden to examples from the past for their tuition, the theme that they treat must ever be new, or they must make it so by an infiltration of thoughts belonging to their own times."[11] Mixing Christian art symbols and realistic detail, Rossetti was chastised by contemporary critics, on the grounds of poor technique and poor intentions. They thought he did not know how to master perspective and an appropriate handling of the Virgin or that he didn't care about doing so. Yet, like much Victorian poetry, and the dramatic monologue in particular, double art goes beyond expressivity and beyond traditional form. It dramatizes how expression and commentary work dialectically in and on a perceiving, embodied mind.[12] Rossetti's painting, exploring figuration in its linguistic and pictorial registers, is far more complex than it initially appears.

Rossetti's *The Girlhood of Mary Virgin* operates on several levels at one time with several kinds of aesthetic intentions. It pays homage to traditional symbology in order to remind the nineteenth-century viewer of a lost past. Rossetti exploits color symbols for virtues: for instance, blue stands for faith, green for hope, gold for charity. Moreover, he draws on objects conveying widely known, Christian-inflected meanings, such as the dove for the Holy Spirit. In addition, he features objects that belong to a typological (predictive) reading of the teleological narrative of Christ's redemptive death, such as the thorns for Christ's martyrdom. Finally, he uses objects that are rarely invoked in these traditional scenes, for instance, a trellis, part of a grape arbor, which signifies the cross and

Christ's passion. One assumes that the trellis isn't original to Rossetti, but that there are precedents in early Christian art; indeed the Rossetti Archive cites a woodcut in the British library as possibly influencing the inclusion of a grape arbor. The treatment of the angel Gabriel is distinctive. He appears as a young boy, according to his proper age in the narrative Rossetti depicts, instead of as anything like the majestic figure with scepter and crown we might recognize from pre-fourteenth-century Annunciation scenes (see Ferguson). Rossetti pays homage not in order to reinstate aspects of institutionalized religion, however. In fact, this example of double art questions the relationship between approaches to the Christian scriptures and inherited ways of reading and assigning meaning. If it evokes a time when the artistic image was viscerally connected to devotion and thought and prayer, it also references—through its incorporation of symbols such as books—a history of scholasticism and commentary that has recorded, but also devitalized, devotion and faith (see McGann, Rossetti Archive).

With his sonnets, Rossetti explores the relationship between the physical body and the mystical one. The first sonnet stresses the secular, temporal realm from which Mary emerges into the moment of the Annunciation. It opens with "This is that blessed Mary"—as a pointer to the painting, but also as a stress on the presentness of childhood—and ends with "the fullness of the time was come." The second sonnet, a holy sonnet, takes up the atemporal realm, reinforced by the conditional "These are the symbols" and more archaic language such as "standeth," "hath said." No longer about the secular, this sonnet focuses on the translation of the Virgin's narrative into spiritual symbols and metaphor.

Only through visual symbolic systems, Rossetti suggests, can we best sense and know the Virgin's mystical importance—through the lily, through the vase, through the lamp, or through the books with names of virtues. In addition, the physical reality of her mother St. Anne and her father St. Joachim in scenes of domestic and arbor work reassert the importance of materiality and literality. Rossetti updates the Christian narrative, while also putting it on trial, so to speak; Rossetti performs a complicated translation. The figures do not have idealized faces (Rossetti's mother modeled for Saint Anne, sister Christina sat for Mary, a handyman Williams posed for Mary's father, Saint Joachim). The setting is an everyday, if well-off, domestic scene; Saint Anne supervises Mary in embroidering a lily (the same lily embroidery that is completed in Rossetti's 1849 *The Annunciation/Ecce Ancilla* DOMINI). The painting offers a predictive reading that also gives a retrospective deeper meaning to that childhood.

Indeed, Rossetti's first example of double art importantly stresses the translation of a material reality into a symbolic one as it explores kinds of sign systems. At the same time, challenging traditional paradigms through transformation of them, Rossetti's double art enacts a cultural critique, questioning the ideological structures and rituals under which an art of idolatry had been produced and consumed. Instead of creating an art that idolizes or makes static the female form or the viewer's gaze, Rossetti uses a variety of cultural sign systems and languages to open up the process of reading and viewing.[13]

A questioning commentary on interpretation as much as a symbolic presentation of a legendary topic, then, *The Girlhood of Mary Virgin* thus exposes the reliance of the Christian narrative, in pictorial and linguistic form, *on* symbolic processes to keep the story of Christ alive. For instance, Rossetti's use of St. Joachim and the grape arbor emphasizes the very process of mystical translation, a change from one state to a different form or substance. On a simple level, St. Joachim's tending of the grapes stands for blood and refers to the future narrative of Christ's physical sacrifice. In turn, the grape will be taken up as the wine of the Eucharist in the institutionalization of the sacrifice. In another instance, the symbolically colored books remind us perhaps of monastery libraries as well as the abstract virtues named, but also raise the idea that we have to go back and read old books to find out what the symbols mean. Thus, Rossetti explores not only kinds of symbology, but also cultural memory. He suggests varied historicized versions of symbols, and notes the process of how something becomes a symbol and can fall away from memory and require clear labeling (virtues on book spines, names on haloes, Latin phrases on the organ and scroll) and directives from sonnets.

The education of the naïve viewer/reader proves as important a topic here as St. Anne's supervision of the innocent Mary in a sacred embroidery, whose import she will not understand until the Annunciation (i.e., the event and Rossetti's painting of the event). Rossetti's handling of the Christian narrative stresses both its power and its lost meanings and purchase in modern times. As long as myths are stable, Rossetti's painting intimates, they last. Rossetti might have agreed with the later anthropologist Bronislaw Malinowski, who claims a myth is "not merely a story told, but a reality lived. . . . It expresses, enhances, and codifies belief; it safeguards and enforces morality" (78–79). When cultural values and assumptions alter, as they did with the nineteenth-century scientific worldview and capitalism, their meanings are diluted and they no longer have a firm hold on our attention. Then we need help to remember and understand them. But they will never resonate in the same way again, Rossetti seems to say; they will remain distanced, unless writers and artists keep them alive and fresh.

Rossetti's handling of perspective in *The Girlhood of Mary Virgin* recalls complexities that Leo Steinberg's analysis of perspective uncovers in Velázquez's *Las Meninas* of 1656.[14] Rossetti's shortened depth of field makes viewing a challenge. It is difficult to figure out the relationship of the floor to the wall to the space behind Mary and Anne, not because the painting is lacking in technique, but precisely because the technique forgoes visual hierarchy. We can't be absolutely sure where the center lies. As Jerome McGann notes, "light in this painting has no source point" (2000, 107). As with Turner's Polyphemus painting with its various light sources, so here, too, it is impossible to point to a single source.

Eyes, which often mark out angles of vision, do not help us fix a central position in this painting. Noticeably, most lead us not to dwell on one object or one body, but out of the frame, as if spirituality drove the gaze, not another person. Indeed, all members of the Holy Family pointedly avoid looking at each other or at the viewer; nor does God's minister engage any human figure. Mary looks, rather glassy-eyed, over the angel's head out of the frame to the left, not at her labor of embroidery. St. Joachim looks up out of the frame more than at the vine in his hand (for that his head would have to be adjusted). The only eyes concerned with the actual activity depicted within the painting are St. Anne's. Although she supervises Mary's embroidery, she also seems unengaged. Finally, the angel looks off out of the frame to the right, not at his lily watering.

If we address the width of Rossetti's canvas as a physical object, taking a measurement side to side, the center of the painting is at the cruciform trellis. According to one kind of viewing, and on one level of meaning, a prediction of Christ's crucifixion is the center, symbolically and literally, of this painting. Mary takes her meaning from that association. Relating that center to the title, her education in girlhood is 'for' something—it prepares her to birth the savior; her life will be shadowed by his death; her name will be honored by his deeds, martyrdom, and resurrection.

On the other hand, if we look to the vanishing point of traditional geometric perspective to find the center, attending to orthogonals, we discover that strong verticals and horizontals—the wall, the trellis, the embroidery, the curtain, drapery, the lily—keep perspective in doubt. The floorboards point us inward but do not align. To be sure, the embroidery stand's foreshortened angle leads the eye back to the dove and what is beyond it, hills and purple shadows. There is some sense of a vanishing point in the natural scene over which, or in front of which, the dove hovers; yet perspective blends with pattern. The eye slows and is arrested.

As James Elkins has pointed out, there are various ways to slow an eye: organic forms (here the haloes or the tree's arch or the white pool shape bifurcated by St. Joachim's middle) can slow the eye trying to move backwards or deeply. He remarks: "when figures occlude lines, or parallax disrupts orderly dimunition, perspective is softened enough to turn the eye loose" (1994, 177). He further explains that frontal planes can affect the eye as it travels into fictive depth, perspective can blend with pattern so the eye moves left and right along a surface, instead of deeply, or orthogonals can be shortened or eliminated (177). Linguistic text within the pictorial text also reinforces this slowing down.

If one focuses on the foreground, where the central figure and education event take place, we find not one but at least two centers, both of which align with heavy verticals rather than with perspective angles that lead the eye towards the background. The straight line of the curtain edge and the embroidery stand pulls the eye to St. Anne. The second strong vertical is the lily, reinforced by the standing position and the wings of the angel Gabriel, which pulls the eye upward. We might think we should dwell on Mary, since the title refers to her. But as in Hunt's *Christ in the House of his Parents,* where the important figure of Christ has to compete for visual attention, composition in *The Girlhood of Mary Virgin* challenges tradition by illustrating that "there are no *a priori* main subjects" (Brooks 125). Mary is to the side, literally.

Viewers are left with an equality of objects in front, in back, and in the middle as the eye travels group to group of details, figure to figure, subspace to subspace. If one does choose a center, as some viewers, including Jerome McGann, do—"the haloed dove locates a vortex, an 'inner standing point'—a conceptual (in several senses) center for all the actions represented in the picture," that center is quickly shown to be located "obliquely in a minor key." The Dove is God's point of view, according to McGann (2000, 109), but also a witty nod to the disappearance in the nineteenth century of God, whom one may yet continue to apprehend through signs (see Miller 1963). So this 'convergence' point is actually a sign and a metaphor pointing to an absence.

By offering a verbal text not only in the sonnets, and not only through his title, but also on the pictorial representations of, for instance, the book titles, the inscribed haloes, and a phrase on the organ to Mary's right—Rossetti also draws attention to multiple levels on which we 'read' and 'translate' cognitively what we see: via words, in an ancient (or modern) language, and not only, as I have mentioned, via Christian color coding, or through material symbols of abstract elements in the Christian narrative. The verbal elements of the painting are designed to provoke thought. Yet the intricate composition and the shifting of literal and metaphorical meanings isolate elements of the scene instead of leading us to an integration and a unifying geometrical perspective.

Steinberg proposes that a profusion of visual centers in one painting creates a "scatter effect" (51) and explains that such multiplicity is often reinforced by groupings of colors in blocks. Rossetti uses the color of fabric to create such a pattern. Blocks of red framing the greens are further enclosed by blocks of white fabric serving to frame the reds and, in reverse, red wings framing the angel's white gown. Yet the shadowed white of Mary's dress, of the angel's gown, and of St. Joachim's sleeves pull our eyes back and forth across the wall separating foreground from background, as much as they may pull us deeply inward towards Joachim, as we work to make sense of the separate, divided units of this painting. The more washed-out colors of the background, in spite of the gold around the dove, seem to insist that the 'real' story (in both senses of the word) lies in the foreground, not in the background, not in the dividing plane of the trellis, not in the symbolics. The sheaf on the floor in front, calling to mind painter's brushes or writer's quills, and not only the palms held during Christ's riding into Jerusalem, beautifully emblematizes the scatter effect. Fronds lead the eye in various directions, while at the same time, they mimic but do not perfectly reproduce a cross. So, depending on how one judges the center, there are at least three or four or five of them.

But what do multiple centers of vision and a verbal profusion do in this painting, and why construct composition in this way? Considering the traditional power and meaning of perspective within the Christian narrative alluded to in this painting, it would appear that Rossetti's disruptions deliberately invite competing centralities, time frames, thoughts, and visions. As Steinberg demonstrates, a painting such as *Las Meninas* is concerned with the role vision plays in self-definition (52), summoning a reader's eye to look not at what the picture shows but at what it beholds outside the frame, a royal couple and the viewer. *The Girlhood of Mary Virgin* concerns itself with the role art plays in the construction of the identity of the sacred and with the sacred identity of the material everyday.

In this regard, it is highly significant that Rossetti not only alludes to levels of interpretation, but paints three levels of interpretation: a living thing (lily), a depiction of that thing (embroidered lily), and that for which they stand, Mary, who is at the same time the artist of the depiction (of herself). The painting arrests and pleases the viewer/reader through its vibrant use of color, but also demands thought from the viewer/reader who must become a kind of translator. In this way, the artist Rossetti may have painted an image without depth, but he does not leave the viewer/reader pleasurably on the surface. Rather, the painting demands that one enter it fully—negotiating levels of meaning, dealing with ambiguous centers, rethinking the subject matter, deciding where to focus. In this way, the viewer/reader is, one might say, cornered. Like Mary, the viewer/reader, once in the scene, is kept busy stitching and being stitched into the visual and linguistic 'story.' This artistic method seems indebted in more ways than one to Browning's interiorization of the reader in "Childe Roland to the Dark Tower Came."

The real world and the symbolic world, here the typological world, encounter each other in the space of the painting. The viewer/reader is invited into the encounter, but not offered a seat. We are asked to keep moving back and forth between sonnets and painting, and back and forth and all around within the image trying to put things together. We do not master this painting; for it constantly masters us. Rossetti shows the irreducibility of painting—and of the Marian materials—to an exploration of traditional vision and traditional interpretation where we face a painting, find the center, and award it meaning.

This is also to say that for Rossetti, this early in his career, painting is not a mere extension of vision. It is material. It calls attention to its own materiality, presenting itself as other than easily assimilable, to vision or to language. It is worrisome to some critics that Rossetti apparently believes in an "essence" of things apart from the mind that perceives them. Rather, the emphasis should fall, in my view, on his texts' exposure of the fact that vision and interpretation are based in historical and cultural conventions.

Complex social operations are assigned to and appropriated by objects, especially objects on display, such as paintings and sonnets.[15] The first sonnet identifies the subject and places Mary historically, geographically, and morally. The second sonnet concerns symbolic interpretation, references writing about Christ, and presents symbology, in McGann's words, as an antique "form of artistic expression and style not a vehicle of religious concepts and ideas" ("Medieval" 98). The fact that these sonnets exist and are pinned to the painting is more important, finally, than their words, which is why they are so unmemorable as poetry and so memorable as directives.

By offering the painting to the viewer through a sonnet that concerns itself with the present moment of viewing, Rossetti shows that interpretation is contingent. Yet importantly, the cultural agency of double art is formed not only in relationship to aesthetics and education of a viewer/reader. Nor is it formed only in relationship to issues of class/capitalism/patronage or to gender in the collective worship of an iconic female figure, whether Mary or an image of Jane Burden Morris. Rather, we must ask how the relationship between poem and painting functions in particular settings.

In any setting, a sonnet pinned to a frame is an object that speaks, not only what it says, but its own objecthood, what it is and what it does. This is part of the point of double art. Poems challenge us with a sense of difficult access, but also, when read, of immediacy. A poem pinned to or written on a frame is more than an inert object; it shapes social relationships, delineates boundaries not only between painting and poem, but also between viewer/reader, language, and the visual. We can't know what this pairing does or means in the gallery or the artist's studio or the patron's home without knowing more about historical processes that shape these places and spaces, differently designated as sites of consumption, creation, labor, leisure, or the domestic. We tend to think of poetry in a book or on a manuscript leaf or in a journal issue or declaimed. Yet what does poetry do when it leaves its ordinary or expected place?

For one thing, the position of the poem on the frame helps position people. And thus the placement encourages social acts in advance of reading it. The disjunction in size between painting and poem matters enormously. It demands an audience take up multiple viewing positions. The viewer/reader must go up close to the painting if he or she is going to read the poem. Later, he or she will likely step back again to see the painting whole. Or, more likely, especially given sonnet directives, the viewer/reader will move back and forth from one viewpoint to another in order to look at specific parts of the painting. Double art also establishes boundaries and connections among viewer/readers jockeying for space to see and read it.

Most readers of poems linger with the words, rhymes, syllables, figures. It is an involved, time-consuming process. Rossetti's selection of the sonnet form is telling. This form itself is dialectical, requiring the reader to make sense of units, of propositions, and of turns and counterturns. Like the painting, it is built in sections. Moreover, influenced by fourteenth-century Italian sonneteers Dante and Petrarch and English Renaissance sonnet cycles, the poem references an entire cultural history about love and the worship of a woman that it brings to the reading and viewing situation. In particular, the sonnet is the main poetic form that moves between the secular and the holy—addressed to a Laura, for example, living and dead, earthbound and spiritual.

Thus, placing a poem on a frame is a form of social communication, marking out the positions of persons who occupy the space, whether servant, guard, patron, guest, or gallery goer. It serves as an invitation and an information piece and an object to view in its own right and it, ideally at least, arrests a viewer/reader. The poem's presence slows the pace of experience and interpretation and, unless the viewer chooses to ignore it, the poem heavily controls how, how long, and in what order one reads the image. Certainly, Rossetti's strategy aids Holman Hunt's idea to create in Pre-Raphaelite work an art requiring a viewer to look at detail, to consider small areas of interest, to produce a thoughtful and even a meditative response (Landow, victorianweb). Literally, the poem takes us into the realm of image. It slows time and demands that we encounter space. Although the poem does not fix meanings, it asks the viewer/reader to think about the image in particular ways, not just view it—and to view the poem as artifact also, not just read it—thus enforcing a mental engagement with image and a pictorial engagement with language.

Rossetti explored various kinds of image/text combinations. Sometimes working in the ekphrasis tradition, he responded to another artist's painting, as in "Sonnets for Pictures," which makes up a celebrated unit of *Poems* (1870). At other times he produced text/image pairings by illustrating another poet's words, as in his contribution to the Moxon Tennyson (1858). But he also produced about thirty combinations with poems and painting by his own hand, combinations which are, for my purposes, the most important examples. Often poems appear written on the Rossetti-designed frames of these pictures or appear in a corner of the paintings themselves or, written on paper, they are attached to the corner of the frame or put on its back. In some cases, the doubles have been lost and, in other cases, texts are alluded to only by picture titles.

At different times, Rossetti seemed to prefer one art medium to the other, depending upon whether he was referring to sales or art.[16] In an 1851 note to his aunt, for example, he labeled painting his "real career" and writing a "minor employment" (Doughty and Wahl 99). Following the famous advice of Leigh Hunt that poetry writing would not allow enough money for a man to "live upon while he is in the flesh" (Doughty 62), Rossetti had given up poetry in his twenties. Later, as is well known, he literally gave it up by burying his verse manuscripts with his wife Elizabeth Siddal in 1862, only to exhume them six years later. A shift in emphasis occurred after the (carefully orchestrated) success of *Poems* (1870): "My own belief is that I am a poet (within the limits of my powers) primarily, and that it is my poetic tendencies that chiefly give value to my pictures: only painting being—what poetry is not—a livelihood—I have put my poetry chiefly in that form" (Doughty and Wahl 749).

We might easily mistake Rossetti here as promoting an eighteenth-century notion of translatability between the sister arts or an ideal of unity. Entire nineteenth-century galleries had been devoted, after all, to pictorial translations of literary texts. It was possible, too, that pairings would offer a fuller, better, complementary imitation of reality. However, quite to the contrary, Rossetti is not promoting that ideal of translation. He offers symbolic recreations of ideas, a kind of antipictorialism and antinarrativizing akin to Blake's and to Turner's. For Rossetti, painting does not attain visionary quality by telling stories, nor does poetry by painting pictures.

If Blake wanted to challenge a dualistic, divided world of opposites as a fiction, including that of visual and verbal, by creating unity from contrariety and not complementarity, Rossetti realized unity was out of the question. The interaction could reference potential unity in which such categories no longer functioned, but never attain it. Where Blake made the reader rhetorically and hermeneutically connect the visual and verbal on the page in his illuminated books, to suture over the gap of a fallen world, Rossetti's double art drew the reader into the painting and words on the wall. At the same time, each emphasizes the impossible gap between the contemporary viewer and situation and the content and form of the art painted and written.

Pairing a poem with a painting, whether side by side, affixed, or by writing on the painting itself, was not in itself an unusual practice.[17] Within a long, expanding, and complex history of the sister arts, Rossetti's double art holds a unique position. In some cases, he creates a *set* of textual and visual materials, rather than a single pair. Each instantiation of a figure/idea such as Mary, or of a particular style of art such as the Venetian, for instance, can serve as one individual perspective. Each dialogic pair or set is one view of what McGann calls in the Rossetti Archive section on doubleworks "an ideal visionary reality." In some cases, two languages are involved, where Rossetti first writes a sonnet in Italian, which he then translates into English, as in the case of *La Bella Mano* and *Proserpina* (1872). Each offers part of a larger history of and commentary on forms of the ideal.

Complicating pendantry, Rossetti does not present pendants or pairs in relays (poem and painting, poem and poem, painting and poem and poem) just to offer multiple views. His very exploitation of two highly complex art forms militates against such a conclusion. Each set is a nineteenth-century attempt (self-consciously belated) to recover a certain historical awareness (early Christian, Roman, Greek, Venetian, Medieval, Elizabethan), in contrast to that of his contemporary moment.

Rossetti aims to bring poetry and painting closer together, without merging them, but also without making one form primary as an explicator of the other. In terms of form, he asks us to see words and letters as graphics and to read paintings as iconic signs. In terms of content, he aims to counterpoint and test major categories by which we order experience: the material and the spiritual, the body and the soul, the everyday and the supernatural, male and female. His texts foreground interpretive systems to pose questions about meaning making.

Perhaps most importantly, Rossetti's art is social in orientation and function, partaking of a heightened self-consciousness, ambiguity, and daring self-exposure, but in the service of serious unmaskings rather than wit or critique. While seeming to universalize the artistic experience, Rossetti's texts show it as a layered experience, that of experiential involvement and that of interpretive involvement, both enabled and limited by historical location, social identity, and embodied experience.

As W. J. T. Mitchell suggests in *Picture Theory*, when theorizing the relationship between verbal and visual languages, one cannot take the relationship for granted. Relations between the two "correspond to . . . an authentic critical desire to connect different aspects and dimensions of cultural experience" (87). We need ask not what the similarity or difference may be between image and text but to what end they are put together at all.[18] Critics differ in how they describe Rossetti's double art and its purpose. Lucien Agosta sees Rossetti as intending an organic whole. Linda Nochlin suggests that the forms explicate each other, but are not locked together in style or content (139–53). Maryan Ainsworth argues that they exist in a "symbiotic" relationship with one art "used to expand the viewer/reader's experience of the other" (4). J. Hillis Miller comments: "each exceeds the other, however they may be deliberately matched." "Each," he goes on, "says more or less than the other, and says it differently, in ways which have only in part to do with the differences of medium. Either may be taken as the 'original' of which the other is the 'illustration.' But then the secondary version is always and can only be, in one way or another, a travesty, a misinterpretation, a distorted image in the mirror of the other art" (1991, 335–36). If we contextualize Rossetti's double art within Victorian poetry of the period and within a resistance to classical Renaissance perspective, we need to see them as interactions between kinds of meaning in which one exposes the other in a continual rearranging of materials and a raising of new questions.

By their assembling and reassembling of words and spaces, lines and colors in conversation with earlier art, Rossetti's texts cultivate a point of view from within the assembled material that is skeptical of that very material. In this example, the scholarship and the iconography that institutionalized Mary as an idealized, or better a de-realized, icon practiced a deformation of feeling. Rossetti selects, instead, the fleshly, feeling girl Mary and carries through with that presentation in his *The Annunciation*.

In his resistance to a Romantic construction of subject and object, Rossetti crafts a poetics in which "the art object itself is drawn into the point of view taken towards the nominal subject" (McGann, Rossetti Archive, Introduction). He explores a dramatized point of view, what he calls the "inner standing point." This is a position similar to what we familiarly know as the poetic space achieved by a dramatic monologue by Robert Browning from whom, McGann suggests, Rossetti learned the technique. In that literary form, the presence of a silent auditor opens a space of irony that dramatizes the speaker's overheard self-revelation. The position of the auditor can be virtually shared by the reader. Rossetti's inner standing point is thus very much related to work by Browning and Tennyson.[19] However, there are significant differences as well.

Rossetti's thoughts about the dramatic monologue, and the dramatized performativity of the lyric "I," do not coincide with those of Robert Browning, despite his admiration for the older poet's use of the form.[20] Rossetti does *not* experiment with point of view in order to distance himself, as poet, from his material. Browning programmatically did so after the poor reception of his highly subjective *Pauline* (1833).[21] Thinking of "Fra Lippo Lippi" (1855) and "Jenny" (1870) may be useful since both feature speakers with whom the author appears sympathetic on the basis of conflicting loyalties. The Browning text, about a fifteenth-century artist, includes the process of an artist making himself part of the artwork.[22] At the end of the poem, Fra Lippo describes a painting he made, *The Coronation of the Virgin*, and notes that the portrait in the corner of the painting is himself "I!— / Mazed, motionless, and moonstruck—I'm the man!" (363–64) and he notes that the scroll with the Latin inscription, which translates to "This is the man who caused the work to be done," refers to him. Although the actual portrait is now thought to be that of the man who commissioned the painting, Browning took it to be the artist. While Browning creates distance between himself and "Fra Lippo," the poem might be said, in expository terms, to describe the situation that Rossetti's poem enacts. "Jenny," set in a whore's bedroom in Victorian London, co-opts the creator and his stand-in, the reader, into the poem's staged action and a series of related moral and ethical problems about commodification of woman, class, separate spheres, and a number of other important social and personal issues of the day. Yet those issues, slightly masked, also can refer to the artist as whore, the commodification of women in Rossetti's art, class divisions between artist and model, types of women in Rossetti's life, and more. Any criticism of the young man in the poem may also be self-criticism; any questioning about goods, value, and money may also be self-questioning.

Instead of sharing distance with Browning, Rossetti, according to McGann, reintroduces "the action of the subjective artist into the critical space of the work" (McGann, Archive, Rossetti Archive, Introduction, 6). Perhaps equally influenced by Turner, who paints so that his viewer experiences sea spray or storm or the center of the sun from *within*, as if in a vortex of waves or living within a ball of light, Rossetti suggests that "an inner standing point" is not the property of one form or one genre, but a requirement of all art. To narrativize, to see and know from without, to describe, is not, according to Rossetti, the function of art, either poetry or painting. As Turner's paintings critique monocular vision in favor of confusions of shapes, color, and light—following more closely how we see and come to know—so Rossetti's double art develops into a style of ornamentation in the 1860s and later that blends natural and supernatural into grotesque arrangements, but they carry a social import.

Ruskin's ideas of gothic grotesque, as developed in *The Stones of Venice* and *Modern Painters,* influenced the Pre-Raphaelites, especially Rossetti. Ruskin noted in a critical statement in *Modern Painters III:* in the art of Turner, Watts, and Rossetti "there may be the dawn of a new era of art in a true union of the grotesque with the realistic power" (5: 137). As Isobel Armstrong has argued, Ruskin's gothic grotesque is a theory of representation "based on a social and not a psychological analysis, seeing psychological experience as determined by cultural conditions" (240). Pater's important essay on Rossetti refers, as well, to the "grotesque" quality of his blend of naturalism and supernaturalism (see Stein 125). Rossetti's sensual double art exposes the construction of myths and ideologies by which we live, shuttles the viewer/reader among them, shows them as prey to history and culture, and shatters their traditional hold on vision and cognition. The loss entailed in this process of destruction produces the very desire and longing for meaning that Ruskin identifies as the most important experience of disturbed modern consciousness.

Rossetti's magisterial and erotic painting *Astarte Syriaca* (1875–77), originally entitled *Venus Astarte*, ostensibly may be considered a subjectless late "stunner," and yet it forces the reader to face the construction of myths, their modern secular blending, and how we experience mixed symbols. Rossetti chose Jane Morris as his model, the spiritual and sensual muse for him during these years. The fact that the word *art* is in the title of the painting, *Astarte,* seems not coincidental. The painting reworks Semitic, Christian, and secular iconography in a critique of religion and in a reinterpretation of the most widely worshipped goddess of all the deities in the Near and Middle East. The painting is not an expression of Venus as much as it is an analysis of the translation of human energies into ecstatic visions and symbols. It drapes the female body with symbology and asks if we lose the embodiment of the body thereby.

Astarte, Canaanite goddess of fertility, war, and love, gazes at the viewer with a steady, all-powerful look: creating, destroying, and preserving. Like numerous counterparts in other eastern cultures, including Ishtar, Isis, and Aphrodite, she is associated with the planet Venus. Rossetti self-consciously includes traditional elements associated with her: her parents, the sun and moon; twining vines, like serpents, illustrating her demonism; angels' hands hovering above her as if she were sprouting horns—illustrating fertility, vertical elements of torches, arms, the girdle tie, and her left leg—emphasizing a phallic power. He emphasizes that she is angelic and demonic, material and spiritual, biologically female, and yet culturally associated with both female and male attributes. The false binaries of sensuality/spirituality and male/female are both addressed by the painting.

A tremendous contrast with Rossetti's earlier work, this painting and those of his later period heighten the interplay between representation and abstraction. In progressively freeing his style from the imitation of realistic detail, and in further materializing abstract ideas, Rossetti exploits further what we saw in *The Girlhood of Mary Virgin*. His painting is not about what we see, but about the process of how symbolic forms come to be, change, and invite new meanings. In this case, he blends religious and secular imagery to reimagine the goddess of love as the body of the flame of desire.

To get the full imaginative sense of Rossetti's Venus, one has to look not only microscopically but also by half-closing one's eyes. She flames like a torch, incandescent at the top as fiery lights fill the nimbus, and she grows upward, like a dark flower blooming on a long stem even as she seems to look down at us. Rossetti garbs her in his favorite color, green, which he has glazed for luminosity, following Titian. Alice Craig Faxon reports that in the iconograpy books to which Rossetti referred, green represented art and hope (193). In another code, the Victorian language of flowers, Astarte's girdle made of roses and pomegranates indicates passion and resurrected life—all meanings Rossetti ascribes to art as well as to his muse.

Commissioned by Clarence E. Fry, the three-quarter length, six-foot high *Astarte* is noteworthy for the pose of the right hand at breast and the left hand with fingers at the genitals, based on the sculpture in the Uffizi, the *Medici Venus*. One of the most celebrated examples of antique sculpture, the *Medici Venus* was mass produced in the nineteenth century as the epitome of beauty. *Astarte Syriaca* may also be a reworking, even this late in Rossetti's career, of the soft and relatively muted, but similarly posed, Raphael *St. Catherine*—the most literally accessible Raphael to all the pre-Raphaelites. For in their student days, the National Gallery, where it hung, shared space with the Royal Academy, as Tim Barringer notes (33). If my conjecture is correct, then *Astarte Syriaca* could also be an homage to Jane as creative artist as well as muse. For in 1860 Jane embroidered St. Catherine in a three-foot tall panel which featured twining flowers, a phallic sword, long, unbound hair, and a face very much like her own.

With regard not to pose, but to location, Rossetti is very likely revisiting Giorgione's *Dresden Venus* and Titian's *Venus of Urbino*—Giorgione places his Venus as a courtesan figure outside; Titian, in an opposite move, places his as a wife figure in a domestic scene. Rossetti alters space realms, perspective, and status by placing *his* Venus in a natural-supernatural sacralized reality, with ministering angels hovering over her. In his preference for primitive, flattened perspective, which he fills with active forms (here torch-bearing, illuminating angels), Rossetti suggests that space is a projection of the consciousness perceiving it *and* of the forms within it as they meet at the surface of the painting. For a painting without depth, it lures the viewer well beyond the surface into unseeable realms.

Most significantly, Rossetti turns Venus to face the viewer with her deep, dark eyes, forcing us to look and leaving no doubt about the alluring depths of her spirituality. He crooks her left hand so that she actively fingers her girdle, leaving no doubt, either, about the intensity or depths of her eroticism. Rossetti revises earlier representations of Venus and Catherine, as he sexualizes the spiritual and elevates beauty and desire to religious heights.

To spiritualize her, Rossetti draws upon the only accepted iconic image in the Old Testament—the cover of the Ark of the Ten Commandments, created, as Exodus relates, out of two angels, hammered in gold and face to face. Ancient commentators speak of the two cherubim on the ark cover as the base of the footstool of God's throne on earth, an allusion reworked in the sonnet. Further, the Bible tells us that God's voice emanates from in between the angels' faces to Moses.

Iconographically the angels here work differently. They do not frame a space from which the deity communicates down to a prophet. In Rossetti's handling they look up, creating an aureole and serving as reminders of the fiery skies from which this earthly goddess emerged. In addition, their hands and bodies frame Astarte—they are immensely physical presences, adding to the erotic, fiery intensity of the image as a whole.

Unlike the Old Testament God's hiddenness, Astarte's face is not turned away, nor is she invisible; as a deity she does not speak through an imperceivable space. Rather, her face speaks directly. Rossetti not only exploits his knowledge of the Old Testament—in one Canaanite tradition Astarte is the consort of the Hebrew God—but, following Blake, as the Rossetti Archive points out, he also draws on the book of Revelation, in which Astarte is both the woman of the sun and the great mother of harlots. Rossetti blends divine and demonic traditions in a re-vision of earthly revelation.[23] His pairing of poem with painting works to this same end of mixing what is normally kept apart.

In writing a sonnet for this picture, Rossetti affixed the sestet to the frame, but dispensed with the octave which was published first as part of F. G. Stephens's 1877 notice of the painting in *The Athenaeum* ("Mr. Rossetti's New Pictures," 14 April 1877) and later rejoined to the sestet for publication in *Ballads and Sonnets* 1881. It is interesting to speculate on why Rossetti used only the sestet with the painting.

ASTARTE SYRIACA
(FOR A PICTURE)

Mystery: lo! betwixt the Sun and Moon
   Astarte of the Syrians: Venus Queen
   Ere Aphrodite was. In silver sheen
Her twofold girdle clasps the infinite boon
Of bliss whereof Heaven and Earth commune:
   And from her neck's inclining flower-stem lean
   Love-freighted lips and absolute eyes that wean
The pulse of hearts to the spheres' dominant tune.

Torch-bearing, her sweet ministers compel
   All thrones of light beyond the sky and sea
   The witnesses of Beauty's face to be:
That face, of Love's all-penetrative spell
   Amulet, talisman, and oracle,—
      Betwixt the Sun and Moon a mystery.

The sonnet opens and closes with one word *Mystery: / mystery,* as if Rossetti aims to fashion a Coleridgean circle poem with its tail in its mouth. *Mystery* colon seems a concept to be defined—the very confusion of images from different traditions before us. *Lo* indicates something wondrous we shall come to know: but when the same word *Mystery* closes the sonnet with a full stop, it suggests both a transformation of meaning during the course of the poem and limits to our visual knowledge of the painting—as mystery remains despite the aspects of definition offered by the poem.

On the level of content, this use of *mystery* at start and finish suggests that all knowing is only ever partial in the face of meanings unfathomable. But at the level of graphics, *mystery* does bridging work in the poem. The word *mystery,* with its reach upward of a *t* and its searching downward *y*'s calls attention both to movement upward into the spiritual realm and downward into the material realm. In its enclosure positioning, *Mystery/mystery* further replicates the torch-bearing angels, as if the repetition of the word serves as the parenthetical markings or the dual ministers of a Beauty positioned between and born of sun and moon.

If the octave, which establishes a genealogy for Astarte, holds descriptive clues for interpretating the painting, Rossetti turns in the sestet to the topic of interpretation itself and to those who worship her. I disagree with the Rossetti Archive that this sonnet "pales" next to the painting, because I view it as equally complex. Ruskin recognized that there was an element of picture in every letter of the alphabet and an element of writing in every picture (Miller 1992, 77). In extending visual theory to language, Rossetti also extends linguistic theory to the image. Notice that the sestet opens with the hyphenated word *Torch-bearing* describing the angels and what they hold. But I would extend that connotation.[24] Astarte is herself a torch. The painting bears and bares her, exposing the viewer to flame. To this end, it seems to me that the **T** is very significant in this sonnet, graphically speaking. A much-used alphabet letter to be sure, *still* it opens three of the last lines and appears thirty-eight times, fifteen times in the sestet. The painting can also be viewed as a set of graphic variations on **T**. Astarte's girdle, in the shape of a T, following the T of her breasts and genitals, is reproduced in the shape that the

Angels make when forming the top of a T—emanating from her head, a T where her figure becomes the T stem.

The sestet not only draws attention to aspects of the painting we may not have noticed, but it *compels* us by drawing us in to the presence of Astarte's face. Drawing on a phrase McGann would use (2000), the painting *spells out,* but by trying to cast a spell on us. McGann has drawn attention to the importance of the pictorial words *draw* and *frame* in Rossetti's sonnets (2000, 71–72). But notice here how the last words of lines in the sestet *compel, see, be, spell, oracle, mystery* both connect and plumb in meaning and in sound the concepts of seeing, being, a spell, and mystery.

If the octave focuses on the goddess, the sestet turns to the viewer—speaking of her worshippers—those who minister to her, those who interpret her meaning, and those who are receptive witnesses to her beauty. These witnesses include not only religious functionaries, in Rossetti's reworking of worship, but painter, poet, the spectator, and the reader. If we let the painting work on us, the sonnet says, we leave penetrated and singed by Astarte's power, imprinted with her face, a living witness to her continuing beauty.

But we also leave with an object. Our experience of the painting becomes an amulet—the portal to a female womb as it ushers us into a different reality than the everyday. It becomes a talisman, something to ward off evil and bring good fortune. And it is an oracle—a shrine in which deity communicates. Rossetti's hyperconscious double art not only compels questions about what we see and know, exposing while exploiting the myths and histories of our knowing, but also demands that the viewer/reader ask what it is to see, to read, to know.

In the second example of late double art, *The Day-Dream,* begun in 1878, Rossetti revises Wordsworthian nature poetry as well as realistic portrait painting of women. Painted again monumentally and again in green, Jane Morris sits this time passively in a natural scene with eyes staring off abstractly and solipsistically, sending the viewer back into her or himself too. She sits slightly sideways, entwined in boughs, as a tree-maiden. Iconographically, she represents regenerate love. The painting's history is especially telling. Originally Jane Morris held snowdrops, but the painting took so long that Rossetti changed the flower to honeysuckle, coinciding with the season in which he completed it. Moreover, first called *Mona Primavera,* emphasizing her as goddess, the painting title became *The Day-Dream.*

Note that in the painting the human and vegetative blend and seem to sprout and leaf together. This fusion is even more apparent in a sketch. Rossetti is not actually creating an icon of springtime or picturing a goddess—hence his title change. Rather, he is representing a woman's dream where the seasons, as in Keats's "To Autumn," can be extended, blended, and even erased through imaginative reverie. This example performs a passionate and erotic blending of the female with nature, as if it would ask where does one begin and the other end? At first glance, it seems a typical, patriarchal construction of woman. Yet, at the same time, it skeptically questions the shaping, even deforming, of the human by the natural and by connection with the natural, asserting the primacy of the human mind over nature.

While the Astarte sonnet was dismembered to put aside the octet's description in favor of emphasizing the sestet's focus on interpretation, this poem's sestet works differently from its octet too.

THE DAY-DREAM
(FOR A PICTURE)

The thronged boughs of the shadowy sycamore
    Still bear young leaflets half the summer through;
    From when the robin 'gainst the unhidden blue
Perched dark, till now, deep in the leafy core,
The embowered throstle's urgent wood-notes soar
    Through summer silence. Still the leaves come
            new;
    Yet never rosy-sheathed as those which drew
Their spiritual tongues from spring-buds heretofore.

Within the branching shade of Reverie
Dreams even may spring till autumn; yet none be
    Like woman's budding day-dream spirit-fann'd.
Lo! tow'rd deep skies, not deeper than her look,
She dreams; till now on her forgotten book
    Drops the forgotten blossom from her hand.

Commissioned by Constantine Ionides from an earlier drawing (1878) where Jane Morris embodies nature in terms of the return of spring, *The Day-Dream* concerns the representation of woman in terms of nature and its relationship to sexuality, both that of the woman and that of the viewer/reader whom her body and eyes desire and who, presumably, desires her. The painting responds directly to a long Idyll by Alfred Lord Tennyson published in his 1842 poetry volume (and illustrated later by

Millais) called "The Day-Dream," which opens:

> O LADY FLORA, let me speak:
> A pleasant hour has passed away
> While, dreaming on your damask cheek,
> The dewy sister-eyelids lay.
> As by the lattice you reclined,
> I went thro' many wayward moods
> To see you dreaming—and, behind,
> A summer crisp with shining woods.

Reminiscent of the situation between speaker and sleeping woman in Rossetti's multiply reworked interior dramatic monologue "Jenny," the painting shows itself to be, like the Idyll, as much about the desires of the reader-viewer as about the object represented.[25] Perhaps we can see most clearly what this example of double art enacts if we reflect on differences between it and another female-in-nature poem, however, Wordsworth's 1798 lyric "To My Sister." There, in a first verse that connects the season, the time, nature, and the human, Wordsworth addresses sister Dorothy—inviting her to put aside her book, her chores, her reason and intellect, to enter a "living calendar" that annuls time, returns to Eden, and rebirths feeling. Unlike Flora, who is asleep, Dorothy is awake, as is the green-gowned lady in the painting The Day-Dream.

Leaving humans out of the octave of his sonnet, Rossetti focuses first on time and the seasons, as if consoling himself that though time marches on, rebirth is possible. In line 6, with a marked caesura, "Through summer silence. Still the leaves come new," he exploits the notion of stillness in terms of quietude/sound, and in terms of duration/time. His juxtaposition of *leaves/come* reinforces seasonal and life changes—filled with cycles of leave takings and comings, births and losses. As with Holman Hunt's representations of the microscopics of nature, which must be read symbolically, the leaves and buds in "The Day-Dream" are echoed in the folds of the green dress and in the red nails and lips of the sitter. We have to read *leaves*, though, not only in terms of kinds of greenery and journeys or departures, but as leaves of poetry and of a sketchbook. Despite regular, expected cycles of birth and death, new leaves sprout even in summer.

However, with the sonnet volta, Rossetti puts aside differences between the seasons and types of inspiration. In the sestet, disavowing a nature poetry of the shadowy sycamore, Rossetti extracts multiple meanings from the word *shade* by which he refers both to leaf cover and to the effect of imaginative reverie. *Shade* means darkness, a shelter, a screen, an unreal appearance, the netherworld, a ghost, a subdued color in painting, a tone in music, a nuance of meaning. Within this kind of deeper than deep, unreal space, Rossetti indicates, spring can be a verb and a noun, dreams can *spring* till autumn. Transcending books, time, and nature, the woman of the sestet immerses herself, but, unlike Wordsworth's Dorothy, she does so *not* to revel in nature and not to lose herself in it. Not nature, says "A Day-Dream," but the human mind in a receptive state enables us to fuse spaces, annul the passage of time, and draw (in both meanings) a spiritual, sexual tongue.

Richard Stein has suggested that "At times, literature is regarded by Rossetti as a form of magic, especially in the rituals of interpretation, where the primary object seems to be the total immersion of the spectator into the mysterious rhythms of art" (203). In *The Day-Dream*, Rossetti plays with surface—making the woman so like the honeysuckle that one expects a transformation like that of a Daphne into a tree at any moment. As the honeysuckle curves and twines and buds, so does she. Yet the two are not equated. More aptly, the relationship is one of simile: as the bird song soars through the leafy core, so the woman may soon voice her pleasure from deep within, unless her dream is also too deep for words. The fact that there is nothing else in this painting but sky pulls us back, though, to the sonnet where the vocabulary of sheathing, budding, core, and tongue intensifies the eroticism but, in turn, again takes us back to the pulsing rhythms of the painting.

Neither organic expressions, nor commentaries on each other, nor distortions of each other, Rossetti's late career double art shows an extreme self-consciousness about form, symbol, mixed media, graphics, viewing methods, interpretive histories, and the conventions of kinds of representation. Locating exteriorly to the double artwork the very process he also wishes his works to perform internally, the negotiation of a gap, he attacks binaries that keep word and image conventionally apart. Representing Mary becomes the conduit for collapsing time in the Christian narrative. *The Day-Dream* offers a dream work, associated by Rossetti with the female, that abolishes the nature/culture divide, and *Astarte Syriaca* blends aspects of the earthly and heavenly realm, while partaking iconically of various antithetical religious and mythic traditions. His examples of double art highlight the circulation of traditional tropes, even as they raise questions about them, modify, and reconceive them in a dialectical manner. Inviting us into realms of secular revelation, they work to critique our reading, viewing, and knowledge as always partial and limited.

CHAPTER THREE

The Photographic Perspectives of Henry Peach Robinson and Lady Clementina Hawarden

So far as photography satisfied a wish, it satisfied a wish not confined to painters, but the human wish, intensifying in the West since the Reformation, to escape subjectivity and metaphysical isolation—a wish for the power to reach this world, having for so long tried, at last hopelessly, to manifest fidelity to another.
—Stanley Cavell 160

Despite examples I have provided in chapters 1 and 2, nineteenth-century visual culture relied heavily upon codes of monocular vision, objectivity, and geometrical perspective.[1] As part of a larger culture of realism dominating the period, these codes not only extended to kinds of painting or to the novel, but also to the new medium of photography. In its early stages, photography promised "a fantasy of perfect re-presentation, a mirroring of the object that surpasses mimesis" (Green-Lewis 25). William Henry Fox Talbot called photography the "pencil of nature," as well as "fairy pictures," "magic pictures," or "words of light." But the Victorians who capitalized on his invention often preferred to discuss it in terms of fidelity, truth, and fact.[2]

Still, from its very beginning, photography's relationship to monocularism and fact was also paradoxical and charged. Traditional theories and practices of vision did not go unchallenged. "For it was photography, in large part," as Lindsay Smith succinctly puts it, "which dramatized the limitations of geometrical perspective as a dominant means of representing three dimensional space in western art" (2). If photography raised the stakes for mimesis by promising an objective duplication of actuality, it also explored borders between realities, created composite realities, and staged partial views.[3]

Nineteenth-century art photography is remarkable for its varied relationships to verisimilitude and to monocular vision. In Jennifer Green-Lewis's view, because photographers such as Julia Margaret Cameron persistently drew on "romantic and literary themes," it offered "the theatrically created suggestion of something other" (61) than an objective reality.[4] To discuss art photography only in terms of its illustration of literary texts, its disavowal of the actual world, or its promotion of an aesthetic, however, is far too limiting. This chapter will take a close look at the ways in which two art photographers of the 1850s and 1860s, Henry Peach Robinson and Lady Clementina Hawarden, engaged with perspective and its relationships to content and to the observer.[5]

While Robinson and Hawarden help destroy the pretence of monocular vision by introducing spatially and temporally contingent views, they do so in radically different ways.[6] Drawing on culturally familiar topics or tropes in order to convey an overall theatrical effect, Robinson wants to hold in place discordant pictorial elements that threaten to move or that, because of a blur, do not match with the rest of the picture. To do so, he creates temporally fixed, allegorical, tableau-like scenes. His photography still adheres to geometric perspective. But, given his reliance on combination printing, it is perhaps more accurate to say that he depends on a set of monocular views that are, paradoxically, not always compatible with each other.

Robinson's photography is both conservative and progressive in terms of fracturing point of view. He juxtaposes multiple negatives and prints to shape a unified pictorial composition.[7] As a result, his work compels viewers to experience an effort that asks them to overlook the demarcations between separate prints yet often calls attention to its disparate contents. Fascinated by seasonal and temporal changes, Robinson connects perspectives, through variously placed figures in his photographs, to specific moments in time. Yet it is significant that Robinson's photographs only thematize the relationship of perspective to time and space.

Even though a unity of effect always remains the objective of a Robinson photograph (see Robinson 1860a and 1860b; Heyert 134; Handy 1–23), his combination prints inevitably raise questions about the nature of reality and the relationship of parts to wholes. Robinson manufactures photographs that press together people, poses, objects, and landscapes that we might never see joined in actuality. Time's passage, as represented in his photographs, thus also becomes unnatural, mythic, rather than real. As a consequence, how we see and who sees what remains as problematic for the postmodern viewer of Robinson's photographs as it had been for informed nineteenth-century viewers.

Unlike Robinson, Hawarden deliberately challenges photography in terms of any claims it might make to verisimilitude. But it is her choice of subject matter and her handling of fluid, Turnerian light and reflection that subverts that verisimilitude.[8] Using a Dallmeyer triple lens no. 1, which increased depth of field, she impacted the photographic medium by evoking figurality and dissolution. Focusing on light as an agent of change in space, Hawarden questions the stability or surety of what the eye sees. Just as her early work with a stereoscopic camera parodied monocularity, her nonstereoscopic images retain a trace of that interest as she continues to show the figure and space in a relationship of mutual recreation. Despite long exposure times needed, her photographs retain a sense of spontaneity, inviting the embodied viewer into the photograph and into a landscape of change. In printing over five hundred photographs of her eldest daughters in her South Kensington, London home, she was not just recording everyday upper-class life in a domestic circle of girls. Nor was she restating a binary between public and private worlds. Rather, Hawarden exposed a complicated relationship among girls, women, daughters, and mothers by exploring the domestic world and its boundaries. Because of her innovative choice of topic, adolescence, not girlhood or childhood per se, her photographs invent a temporal landscape and explore *kinds* of space—psychophysiological, imaginary, and social.

HENRY PEACH ROBINSON AND EFFECTING THE WHOLE FROM PARTS

Combination or double photography, begun by Oscar Gustav Rejlander (1813–75) but achieving immense popularity at the hand of Henry Peach Robinson (1830–1901), was undertaken, paradoxically, in the service of a greater fidelity to nature. Its aim was not to break the visual field, but rather to select details and position parts in order to fashion a more faithful whole. Yet, by shaping a preconceived effect in a viewer, fidelity no longer meant a faithful objective realism. Carefully chosen gestures, expressions, poses, costumes, and locations were guaranteed to elicit predictable effects from the nineteenth-century viewer. Mixed notices of some of Robinson's most popular prints confirm, however, that viewers hardly responded as uniformly as he had expected.[9] The photographer's highly subjective choices of placement created, it would appear, an equally subjective array of reactions.

Combination printing initially developed because the long exposure time needed for early photographs had called attention to the instability of the object. Rejlander notes that Robinson's first use of more than one negative came about when he could not "get a gentleman's figure in focus, though he was close behind a sofa on which two ladies were seated."[10] Other photographers reported the difficulty of photographing the moving sky and a desire to add natural-looking backgrounds. Early photographic materials, in addition, were sensitive to blue and therefore the sky would often reproduce with a light tone—if not with what Robinson called "a smudge" (1869, 192). Robinson became highly adept at replacing not only sky and figures, but also sections of foliage, backgrounds, and objects.[11] Classical training in art taught him to believe in "immutable laws" of contrast, unity, repetition, balance, and arrangement (the best arrangement was by pyramid and diagonal). He strove to raise photography to the status of painting. Maintaining that a combination photograph should never aim to stray from the truth of nature, he cautioned photographers that "[n]o two things must occur in one picture that cannot happen in nature at the same time" (1869, 198). Yet his naturalism was based in deception in order to garner a dramatic effect.

Robinson's very first combination print, "Fading Away" (1856) (figure 2), printed from five negatives, was exhibited at the Crystal Palace in 1858 and mass-produced for shop windows. It garnered instant fame partly because it tricked the public into thinking it was a spontaneous shot and partly because it treated a difficult, controversial topic, the death of a young girl from consumption. But, undoubtedly, it was also successful for its eliciting shared sorrow between the figures and their viewers. Prince Albert was so taken with "Fading Away" that he bought a copy of the photograph and placed an order for every subsequent combination print that Robinson produced.

For a simple combination photograph, a photographer might make prints from two different negatives, cut out parts of the prints, paste them on a photographed background, and then photograph the resulting collage all over again. The more advanced combination printing practiced by photographers such as Robinson relied on sketching a scene first; making photographic studies of parts of the scene; posing a number of models in groups; printing a large number of negatives, from five to thirty; then choosing, cutting, and arranging image parts along joining lines, which were assembled to be photographed for a final print. For purposes of composition and to capture the right effect, the heads of models could be cut off and sutured onto the bodies of others, just as the sky or landscape of one scene was scissored out and pasted into the final picture.

Figure 2. Henry Peach Robinson, "Fading Away," composite photograph made from five negatives, 1858; George Eastman Collection, Rochester, New York

Robinson's "Autumn" (1863) offers a particularly interesting example of the more complicated practice. Filled with puzzling elements, it serves a pastoral ideal of reality and hence may easily be dismissed as a sentimental distortion of a season and place. Our first glance of grouped figures with cut sheaves becomes more problematic upon a closer inspection of the composition's joined parts. The sheaves do not realistically belong in this forest setting. If laborers, the figures are hardly grain cutters; their attire and their postures suggest that, instead, they may be farm workers on an outing who have decided to pause and rest to take in a river view.

The traditional meanings for the season of autumn evoked by this composition, harvest and transience, are equally unstable. Although we can't be sure that Robinson had in mind Keats's ode "To Autumn," the photograph aims to prompt thoughts and images of a Keatsian fullness. The beauty of river foliage and the languid poses struck by the female figures and by a solitary male viewer suggest the celebration of a "soft-dying day" (Keats, line 25). Harvested wheat is placed next to young people, intimating a contrast between immaturity and ripeness as in integral component of nature's life cycle. Yet the group of figures is set against a background that looks as if drawn by a young Turner or even Constable. A light-struck body of water and a distant countryside beckon as prospects to another realm.

Robinson's composition thus is far more complicated than it may appear. The photograph positions four young women and a boy in a wooded, pastoral scene looking in different directions. The three sheaves of wheat at the lower border of the photograph anchor the picture. Although the figures were photographed in two groups, the four on the left in one shot and the single figure on the right in another, their postures divide the picture triply with the two figures on the left lounging and sitting, the two girls in the middle standing, and the single figure on the right curled up in a more compact sitting position than the girl on the left. Spatial groupings and the figures' differing visual perspectives thus help reinforce the sense that Robinson is allegorizing three temporal perceptions associated with the season of autumn: past, present, and future. One group looks off into the distance, one looks at other figures nearby in the present situation, while the single figure's eyes are hidden. The dying of the year is always a poignant moment for reflection back on the glories of summer, for holding onto the cider press of fall, and for anticipating the future unknowns of winter.

Robinson exploits shadow as much as compositional placement to reinforce contrary perspectives. The important single figure seated in the right foreground is in shadow with her back to the viewer. On the one hand, she and the dark foliage behind her help steady the picture; on the other hand, her dark shape lends a note of ominousness to the scene. Since we cannot see her face and eyes, she may well be an older woman, and not a young woman, after all. Allegorically, she may represent Age, Fate, or, in Keats' terms, a carelessly sitting Autumn herself. Here she reclines not on a granary floor or by a cider-press, as in "To Autumn," but on a mossy bank. Nevertheless, she is "like a gleaner" or one who "with patient look" watches the passage of time (Keats, 19–22). If she is a figure for time passing or time past, the boy and girl on the left (the boy with a sense of immediacy in his pose and face and the girl with a pose of languor), seem to represent the present moment, whereas the girls in the middle who are brightly lit and look into the distant prospect beyond, may represent the future. Yet, given that the shaded figure looks in the same direction, that distance may also represent an afterlife, attainable only after crossing the this-worldly reality in which all five figures are situated.

Robinson describes one viewer of "Autumn" as complaining about the divergences among the figures, that "these figures did not agree with one another; that the light fell on them from different quarters; that the perspective of each had different points of sight; and that each figure was taken from a different point of view" (Robinson 1869, 199). This complaint, however, is precisely the point. We might critique the photograph for its artificiality and its contrivance, yet Robinson's introduction of varied perspectives and light sources creates a tension and drama within the image designed to be imitative of the multiple effects of autumn on the human psyche.

Photographs such as "Autumn," "Sleep" (based on the children of "Tristram and Iseult"), or "The Lady of Shalott" evidence Robinson's thorough knowledge of nineteenth-century painting, literature, and illustration. His similarly well-grounded, numerous writings on photography show him to be in dialogue with both earlier and contemporary British and continental culture. He is especially conversant with Romantic poetry, Ruskin's art theory, the masters of engraving, Pre-Raphaelitism, and the artist he hails as "our greatest master," Turner (Robinson 1869, 150).

Robinson's photographs pander to the hunger for pictorial narrative in the paintings, dramas, novels, and poems devoured by the elite as much as by the masses in nineteenth-century British culture. Art photography and historical reconstruction photography also borrowed from the available cultural codes of narrative, including intertexts and "a conventionalized language of facial expression, pose, and gesture, sometimes remote from the gestures of contemporary life, but not narrowly bound to tradition either" (Meisel 5).[12] Robinson drew on both the impulse to illustrate and on this theatrical language of physiognomy and the body. His photographs are static and theatrically posed, often artificial looking, sometimes featuring a single figure and often a tableau. They freeze a significant moment in time.

In this sense, and perhaps in this sense only, his work bears comparison with the paintings of John Everett Millais. Distinguishing between narrative accounts in poetry and painting versus those that concentrate the whole story in the "turning point," Meisel places Tennyson and Millais in the latter camp (35). In their art, he says, story becomes "a situation, a moment of poise, as in some of Millais's story paintings; a moment of epiphany as in some of Hunt's" (35).

Robinson's 1863 "Autumn" thus seems worth connecting to Millais's masterpiece *Autumn Leaves* of 1856. Employing dark forms against a light background, Millais sets the scene at twilight. The four prepubescent girls, all lovely, stand in a strikingly lit scene with a bold, solidly defined red scarf on the youngest child at the right foreground balancing the evanescent smoke that drifts off to the left. While the girls represent youth and beauty, the clouds, smoke, and burning dead leaves evoke the inevitability of the seasons, culminating in death. So, too, the girls, innocent and blooming now, are colored already by twilight and will die. The hand of the tallest girl, at the center of the picture, blends into the dark shadows surrounding it in a central statement of encroaching darkness. Unlike Millais's historical or illustration paintings, it bears drama and sentiment but no external narrative.

Millais had been reading Tennyson's *The Princess* (1847) while painting *Autumn Leaves*; his painting references sentiments from the first lines of the deeply moving song of Part IV:

> Tears, idle tears, I know not what they mean.
> Tears from the depth of some divine despair
> Rise in the heart, and gather to the eyes,
> In looking on the happy Autumn-fields,
> And thinking on the days that are no more. (lines 21–25)

Despite the absence of color in Robinson's photography, so central to meaning for the Pre-Raphaelites, Robinson draws in the viewer, as Millais does, via mood and subject. Like Millais's paintings such as *Autumn Leaves* or its pendant *Spring*, Robinson's photographs sacrifice a sense of the real to allegory and a feeling of depth to paper doll or frieze-like flatness. While Millais's figures look at the viewer directly or at each other, Robinson's do so to a far lesser degree. In his photograph "Autumn," the perspectives he introduces set up varied and contingent views, which do not serve only to bind the whole, but which also serve to fracture it. Moreover, he negates or neutralizes the presence of the observer, who is both invited into the picture and at the same time, facing the back of the darkened, seated female, shut out.

Consequently, the relationship of the observer to Robinson's photographs is also doubled. The observer is both pulled in and pushed away by photographs that demand subjective mediation and yet also hold out for an ideal objectivity. Appearing as a material object that one views in a gallery or as a set on stage, the photographs offer neither a lived reality nor a scene in which the viewer can fully partake.

Even when barely noticed, the joins of Robinson's photographs contribute to this tension. Aware of himself as a manufacturer of reality, despite his credo of fidelity to nature, Robinson cautioned against sloppy workmanship in joining the negatives of combination prints.[13] Because combination photograph prints were contact prints with no way of enlarging certain parts to blend better with other parts, some of the joining spaces or lines are still visible, as cracks in the visual field. Moreover, forms and distances were not always accurately proportioned. Geometric perspective was difficult to maintain: a figure might be too large to fit properly, a landscape edge might not blend in smoothly, and, above all, multiple light sources or competing vanishing points might call attention to the surreal nature of the blended whole.

This handling of a geometric perspective is not unlike that exhibited in the quasi-medieval flatness of Dante Gabriel Rossetti's early paintings (see *The Girlhood of Mary Virgin*, chapter 2). But Robinson's pasting of parts to make a more effective and truthful whole has a different result in photography than similar techniques in Pre-Raphaelite painting. Precisely because photography seems to tell us we are looking at the spontaneous real, the ingenious deceptions of combination printing are unsettling to viewers who become aware of the method. In many cases, one can go further to say that since Robinson produces images taken from different negatives, his photographs could be unsettling even to viewers unaware of his methods.

Robinson attempted to defend his techniques in a paper he presented to the Photographic Society of Scotland on March 16, 1860, nine years before he wrote an entire book on the subject. When his lecture "On Printing Photographic Pictures from Several Negatives" appeared in *The British Photographer* (2 April), it raised an outcry. For it had punctured the illusion of his viewers when he described how he had joined one model's head to another's body and how he had put a bank he covered with ferns and flowers into a birch yard "about fifty feet long by twenty feet wide" (1860b, 2). At the foot of the bank, he revealed, a hole into which waste water flowed from a print-washing apparatus helped him to form a river. Accused of having created a "patchwork" school of photography (L. Smith 103), Robinson replied by insisting that he practiced a higher art of composition: "I can get nearer to the truth for certain subjects with several negatives than with one" (1860a 3).

"Fading Away" (1858) (figure 2), his most famous "composition," illustrates the tensions that Robinson's art sought to exploit as well as to efface. The central figure of a dying young woman dominates the foreground. By having female relatives flank her, Robinson dramatizes emotion inherent in the spectacle of death and in the solemn faces we see. The very act of choosing two figures to frame the prone body evokes a motif from gravestones. A shadowy stool in the foreground is left close to the young woman and her female attendants—perhaps inviting the observer to move the drapery on it, sit, and wait. The middle plane is occupied by a dark male figure looking out the window. A yet further ground, seen through the window, of moon, water, and sky, is linked with shimmering light and the unknown.

Although "Fading Away" clearly is meant to picture an upper-middle-class domestic circle, it is also importantly universalizing through its conventional posing. The central scene reiterates other Victorian depictions of domestic clusters around a sickbed, around a hearth, and sometimes, in the cult of the dead, around an open coffin. At the same time, "Fading Away" evokes other photographs and paintings that feature a lovely young girl in white. The props in "Fading Away" are also carefully chosen. Reading has faded (the woman on the left holds a book she has closed), flowers are fading, the light in the sky is crepuscular. Importantly, Robinson chose verses from the poem "Queen Mab" by a youthful but morbid Percy Bysshe Shelley to go with the photograph: "Must then that peerless form / . . . That lovely outline, which is fair / As breathing marble, perish?" (lines 12 . . . 17).

The selected passage calls attention to the death of a girl so beautiful that she looks as if she is art come to life and returning to non-being. Despite photography's association with permanence, "Fading Away" highlights mobility. If combination printing allows pieces to be lifted, discarded, or re-pasted, it also allows human forms to be literally removed from their original settings and placed into alternate realities. Robinson's photographic method of cutting and pasting can be enlisted to call attention to transience or movement as much as to the stasis of an epiphanic moment lifted out of the maelstrom of time.

Who is the male figure turning his back on the three women in the foreground? His removal from the dying young woman suggests that he is not an attending physician but a relative, perhaps an older brother, or even an uncle, if not a father. He may thus be part of a family circle which seems to include the mother on the left and an older sister on the right, though naturally these identifications are born of coded cultural expectations and not certainties. On the other hand, if the photograph is a commentary, in part, on the spread of consumption as a disease, the pose of the man, turned away from the central event, with left hand raised to head, may indicate the sense of waste and failure felt on the part of a physician who stands helplessly by, waiting only for the last breath before he must make yet another house call. Lastly, the gentleman may be a Christian clergyman. If a doctor ministers to bodies that are transient, a clergyman ministers to souls entering another world. In the photograph this prospect of another reality, as in "Autumn," is depicted with the water, light, and luminosity, towards which the man has turned. No matter what the man's role in the drama of death before us, we do not know if he is a believer or a doubter. We are not sure if the young girl will float into another reality or not. Robinson does not show us. The photograph could as well be entitled "Turning Away" as "Fading Away."

Significantly, as Lukacher suggests, we as viewers are facing the same way as the photographer and the male figure, but the object in each case differs: the photographer sees a domestic scene of waiting for death, whereas the male figure turns towards the landscape and the light source outside. The observer of the photograph thus is invited to look at and to look beyond. Equally interesting, just as the photographer would be draped between lens and curtain, the male figure stands between dark curtains before the glass window (Lukacher 33) as if reduplicating the position of the photographer's view.

As the viewer stands in the position of the male figure and the photographer, though, nobody looks back at us or at each other. In an earlier chapter, taking direction from Leo Steinberg's treatment of *Las Meninas*, I suggested we examine internal gazes in Rossetti's *The Girlhood of Mary Virgin*. The narratologist and cultural critic Mieke Bal (1991, 158–60) calls internal looks "the focalizers of an image." She explains: "If an external focalizer or spectator can look in the same way at the same thing as a focalizer in the picture, then our identification with the image will be strong" (Bal quoted in Rose 2001, 44; see also Bal 1997, 142–70 on the dynamics of focalization in "every visual text" [170]).

In "Fading Away," this identification process is complex. Whereas the two women looking at the dying girl are the central focalizers, drawing our attention to her, the man at the window exerts a strong counterpull as he looks away, out the window. Like the darkened female figure in "Autumn," this man turns his back to us. We are not sure what the man sees when he looks. Nor can we know if his eyes are open or shut. Does his hand cover his eyes? We have no idea where he gazes or what he sees. If we move from the women's gaze and the dying girl to identify with the man, then the basis for identification hinges on issues of subjective thoughts and a looking beyond. Looking beyond to a future or a past is also a turning and looking away from the central present scene; this impulse passes to the viewer. In other words, the man's gaze injects distance into the viewing as well as into the scene.

The formal innovation of combination printing started by Rejlander and developed in the tableaux rituals of Robinson was an experiment whose subject, finally, was not time, the seasons, ritual events, transience, or beauty. For combination printing inaugurated a new handling of photographic subject, a new language of printing, a new responsibility for the observer to read parts, and a new way of observing parts and the whole of an image. Robinson's method challenged many of the cultural presuppositions about photography: its immediacy, its objectivity, its fidelity to the real, and its unity. Symbolically speaking, Robinson's "Fading Away" concerns not only the passing of a beautiful young woman, but also the transition of a way of representing reality itself—from a mastered single field of vision to another, more fragmented mode in which parts and perspectives fissure the whole.

THE DOUBLE PERSPECTIVE OF LADY HAWARDEN

The photographs that Lady Clementina Hawarden (1822–65) took between 1857 and 1864 in her home in South Kensington, London, ninety percent of which are held at the nearby Victoria and Albert Museum, have elicited increasingly avid attention in recent years.[14] Women scholars especially have been fascinated by the five hundred photographs of her daughters (see Barlow; Ramirez 1; Mavor all; C. Armstrong; Dodier 1999, 10; Rose 2002, 103 and 2000, 557). The luminous intensity of this collection of albumen prints registers Hawarden's demand for and achievement of an embodied vision, but also confirms her ability to speak deeply to women about aspects of femininity and female roles.

In her own day, Hawarden's photographs were already celebrated for their technique and subject matter by such well-known photographers as Oscar Gustave Rejlander and Lewis Carroll (who bought several for his albums). Public acclaim came with silver medals from the Photographic Society of London in 1863 and 1864, when Hawarden exhibited her photographs under the group titles "Studies from Life" and "Photographic Studies." Overlapping social circles with James McNeill Whistler and his brother-in-law Francis Seymour Haden may account for the possibility that Hawarden's photography influenced mood painting and the Etching Revival (Dodier 1999, 98–104; Lawson; Haworth-Booth 113). In modern times, art journalists and art historians have stressed the doubleness at the heart of her work, praising "her awareness that fancy and fact coexist in a photograph," and noting that "this coexistence is at the very heart of the photographic enterprise" (Grundberg 1990, 1; and see Lawson 8).[15]

Hawarden's early experiments in photography while still at the family estate of Dundrum, County Tipperary, involved a stereoscopic camera and prints. Embracing the stereoscope's handling of space and depth, she quickly advanced beyond the monocular Cartesian model of scene and traditional perspective. Prominent in her London indoor photographs, examples of which I shall discuss, are her eldest daughters, especially Clementina and Isabella, often dressed in light colors or white, whether in contemporary dress or older costumes. Hawarden surrounds them with abundant and aberrant natural light and shadow; uses swaths of full skirts or long muslin or net curtains as props; sometimes positions them near stone or wood barriers and balustrades or windows; and frequently features objects such as a vase, a concertina, or a box with multiple drawers.

Hawarden's fascination with doubling is evident in over a hundred photographs in which she positions her daughters with a mirror or reflective window glass. Again and again, her pictures establish a close, sometimes intimate, sororal relationship between paired figures. When using two figures, she frequently reinforces oppositions with dark and light dresses or stresses likeness and mimicry by counterfacing two girls with glass between them. She very rarely uses close-ups and only occasionally features a London cityscape as a blurred background.[16]

Most critics agree that the photographs explore a time of a girl's life, an in-between temporal phase here spatialized as a border land, on one side of which lies girlhood and on the other side of which lies womanhood.[17] Moreover, this intermediate realm, half real and half fantastical, is observed through a mother's collaborative and modeling eyes. By *collaborative,* I mean that the girls have collaborated with their mother—they have modeled for her, they have modeled themselves after her, and they have helped with printing. The collaboration is emotional, as well as artistic, and stems from a same-sex maternal–daughterly intimacy.

The uniqueness of Hawarden's work becomes apparent when placed in a larger context. By relying on family members as models she often dressed in costume, Hawarden drew on conventions of the day practiced by other professional and amateur photographers such as Cameron, Rejlander, Robinson, Emerson, Munby, and Carroll, who dressed friends, servants, and family. The vast number and obsessive repetition of similar poses, figures, and props also connects Hawarden to the penchant for documentation or classification that marked the early staging of photographs as a kind of museum or a mode of display (Roberts 26).[18] Hawarden's photographs thus participate in what Michel Foucault would identify as the interlacing of discourses and technologies aimed at the invention of new subjectivities whose reduplication could control individualization.

Yet, despite her participation in this inevitable process of modernity and her dependence on similar ideological forces, Hawarden's photographs are also remarkably different from those produced by her contemporaries, both amateurs and professionals. The enormous emphasis on narrative in the Victorian period, which affected, as we have seen, both Pre-Raphaelite art and Robinson's photographic combinations, is markedly absent in Hawarden's photographs. They stand apart as programmatically nonnarrativizing and willfully resistant to narratives imposed upon them.[19] Hawarden shatters nineteenth-century expectations for story and works against a reduction of the image to language. This seeming resistance may, of course, be partly a matter of the sketchy historical record (perhaps a Hawarden diary or a set of letters is lost), but within the photographs themselves, she rarely references intertexts by alluding, as Robinson did, to literary productions by poets such as Tennyson, Arnold, and Shelley. Moreover, she does not write about her photographs, gives them no individual titles or dates, and rarely identifies them on their reverse sides with text or code. If Hawarden resists satisfying such a cultural imperative, she also prevents a viewer from constructing some story *about* her photographs. Critics have trouble identifying a story or naming their topic. Indeed, Dodier (1999) and Haworth-Booth, thinking of her stress on form or thinking ahead to Whistler, perhaps, go so far as to call them subjectless. As I will later argue, although in this context *subjectless* refers to content, it may also be taken otherwise. Hawarden's photographs also shatter the perspectiv-ally based stability of a subject-spectator, thus drawing attention to the mobility of vision and to multiple and divergent spatial views.

In terms of content, Hawarden's images almost insist on remaining untitled. According to Gillian Rose, Virginia Dodier's Victoria and Albert Museum catalogue of the photographs by number, probable date, and identity of family members may actually prelabel the archive for any new researcher in ways that are counter to the intentions of the pho-tographer (Rose 2000). As we know from Allan Sekula, the construction of a photographic archive is itself influential in shaping interpretations (1986; 1987). Carol Mavor's personal captions of Hawarden photographs reproduced in her book *Becoming* perform an even greater disservice by misleading unwary or casual readers who, coming upon them for the first time, may incorrectly attribute such titles to the photographer herself.

In other photographs of the period, such as Cameron's or Carroll's, costumes offer clues to the stories, poems, or fairy tales any given pho-tograph illustrates. Cameron's invited reproduction of scenes of Tenny-son's *Idylls of the King* or Carroll's and Robinson's staging of "Little Red Riding Hood" stem from an urge to illustrate that is not paralleled in Hawarden's repertoire. Nor is her use of costumes related to achieving the single dramatic or scenic effects that Robinson had sought to pro-duce in his work. Recent Hawarden critics have been eager to identify costumed types such as Mary Magdalen, Joan of Arc, or fallen women in her photographs; they have claimed to see emblematic embodiments of coded gestures or physiognomies (see Dodier 1999; Mavor; Lawson). Yet such identification can hardly be made with the same certitude that allows us to unravel layers of meaning in Robinson's "Sleep" or "Fading Away." Even a full knowledge of the sophisticated codes through which the Victorians read surfaces in physiognomy and theatrical gesture is of little help in decoding photographs that defy narration. Dodier seems to acknowledge this difficulty when she allows that "the images in some of these groups may have been linked by narratives that are no longer explicit" (1999, 13). By implying that personal narratives may have been lost to history or were based on private theatricals or made-up stories, she tacitly acknowledges her need to pin down the nature of Hawarden's unusual artistry, and yet she also reveals the elusiveness of that artistry.

When Hawarden displays her eldest daughters, it remains mys-terious as to why she is putting them on display or how she might link photographs that cannot be put into a discernible sequence. Her relationship to young women is unlike Cameron's or Carroll's.[20] If the photographs do offer visual cues of courtship rituals, or of literary, historical, or mythic characters, they do so only to point up young women's reliance on or playing with cultural narratives of romance or heroism as an aspect of identity shaping, rather than serving as specific illustrations to feed the public taste. Hawarden, I would argue, encourages a playing with a range of cultural narratives, through pose and dress, and that fact is far more important than naming them.

Although each extant photograph is but a single print, with the plates lost or destroyed, Hawarden repetitively turns to her eldest daughters. The photographer-mother seems keenly interested in generation and reduplication. (It is probably significant that few photos exist of her only son.) The camera revels in her eldest daughters' poses and reveries. Hawarden seems entranced by (or nostalgic for?) adolescent secretiveness, sexual flirtatiousness, and narcissism; she always betokens an awareness of the larger adult world that encroaches on youth and beckons an egress. Hawarden's photographs of female meditation point to her understanding of the private worlds older girls crave and need; her photographs of sisters embracing speaks to her understanding of sororal relations, whether she documents closeness or not. Her camera is drawn to boundaries, social markers, and differences. She relies on contrasting realities such as outside/inside, dress/undress, dress-up/contemporary fashion, costumes and role play/self-identity. Although we see the camera box in one photograph, we have no more than one photograph extant of the photographer herself. Even that one image may be her own sister and not herself.

Perhaps this is why the photographer is not in the photographs; versions of her already exist in the photographs. Her daughters replicate aspects of their mother—in looks, in qualities, and, according to a cultural narrative, in their future role—and she, in turn, duplicates and reduplicates them in photographs, reproducing them in reflection doubly, while revisiting her earlier selves by photographing them.[21] The fact that Clementina's eldest daughter is named Clementina reinforces this emphatic sense of doubling and redoubling. Taken together, the photographic pairs, series, and sets serve as prefilmic explorations of the rituals and transitions of puberty and heterosexual desire through the lens of the mother/daughter relationship, which prepares daughters to move through the window into the outer social world, where they become women.

Taking photographs in two rooms on the second floor of her South Kensington home with views to the east and south of Princes Gardens and of communal gardens between her home and Princes Gate to the north, Hawarden attends to different external and internal sources of light. Unlike a painter, Hawarden does not covet the unchanging light from a northward-facing studio but is drawn, instead, to the variations and streams of a southern light that "suffuses and dissolves form" rather than making it emerge (Lawson 7). In her use of multiple light sources, Hawarden thus resembles Turner and the Impressionists; in her choice of single or small clusters of female figures, she may be compared with Rossetti and Whistler.

Hawarden explores depth in terms of how light and its shadows shape our view of physical bodies which appear as forms, patterns, and substances.[22] Showing light as both a creator and agent of vision, at the same time, she playfully introduces the viewer to the interplay of surfaces and depths, exteriors and interiors. Although in this chapter I don't have space to analyze the many types of photographs she produces, I would suggest that she often toys with the viewer in those images that present us with boxes and drawers closed, but fingered or eyed, and those in which her daughters are half-undressed. Both of these seem to draw attention to concealment and to the limits of both optical fidelity and language as avenues to knowledge.

Hawarden notes traces of moving light balanced by shadows when she shows light patterns on a skirt or a bed cover, as in a photograph of Clementina reclining with a jug, table, and mirror as props. She explores reflections on glass and uses the window as the source or frame or reflector of light. Perhaps the most memorable of such photographs is a stereoscopic one that places Clementina outside, seemingly about to close a tall rectangular window or step in through it—she is emerging from and with the source of light into a lesser interior brightness. Sometimes the mirrors themselves seem to emit light, as in a photograph of Isabella in a fancy dress in front of a mirror that showers light on the reflection of her hair. Literally highlighting transitions and boundaries, Hawarden exploits photographic blurring of face or hand or sleeve into light itself, as in the photograph of Clementina kneeling before a window or in one which captures the half body of a sister next to Clementina in pants. Figures or faces blend or dematerialize into the source of vision, natural light.[23] This makes the photographs, as Gillian Rose argues, especially attractive to theorists of performative femininity—the "women are both there as women and not there at all" (Rose 2002, 106). The photographs are "subjectless" not only in terms of identifiable content, but also in terms of a sense of presence.

It is perhaps by chance or choice that the textured drawing-room wallpaper itself serves as a commentary on kinds of light sources. Installed a year or two after Hawarden started taking photographs, it features gold stars on a gray background (Dodier 1999, 35). While a fashionable pattern of the time, it is noteworthy that the chosen pattern should replicate celestial bodies that emit light and that the star is also a Marian emblem, signifying virginity.[24]

One of the most notable aspects of the photographs, besides Hawarden's fascination with light, is the rigidity of the terrace stone which extends to the facades of outdoor buildings and the ceiling-to-floor window frames. In some photographs the figures seem to float, even when seated, but are counterbalanced by stone or wood, frames or sills. The use of barriers and boundaries as common backdrops and our cultural attitudes about the lives of Victorian women have led at least one scholar to speak about Hawarden's photographs as visions of restriction or the desire for escape from the domestic sphere (Ramirez 51). The fact that barriers, balconies, balustrades, and borders exist in some of the photographs is surely significant, but I wonder to what extent separate spheres are being binarized in these photographs.

If one considers a different frame for the reading of the photographs, as a set or series about adolescence, maternity, and womanhood, then they document the things girls and young women do at home before they leave their maternal home to become mothers and wives themselves. Whether or not this is a politically progressive set of documents seems to me beside the point; mothers do not always agree with dominant cultural narratives while at the same time feeling they must prepare children to perform a role in society.[25] Life at home with mother becomes not only a playground but a training ground for the very upper-class world in which Hawarden's daughters were expected to function. The sequence of photographs of her daughters—and ultimately it seems to me their ordering is immaterial because they can endlessly substitute for themselves—exists as a recording of such a charged preparation for a future "life." At the same time, the forward-looking photographs also offer a nostalgic look over the shoulder to the photographer's own past lives *and* provide a record for the photographer to keep when her daughters have departed.

It is worth pausing a moment to reflect upon photographic sequences and their public exhibition. During the years in which Hawarden displayed her work, established methods of presenting photographs included grouping them in exhibition frames or albums (Dodier 1999, 13; 57 illustration of a South Kensington exhibition). Such sequences could convey panels that formed a story or merely cluster similar themes. Robinson is credited with creating the first sustained photographic 'story' in his famous 1858 four-print sequence, displayed together, the *Story of Little Red Riding Hood.* The absence of individual or group titles makes Hawarden's London exhibition titles "Photographic Studies" and "Studies from Life" all the more meaningful. In her explanation of *studies,* Dodier suggests the modesty of unretouched and domestic drawing room "exercises" that make no claim to greatness. For her, *Studies* seems to refer to a stage of artistic process, a preparation for a larger work, and something relatively small and intimate (44). This meaning can be extended to imply that Hawarden executes her works for the sake of acquiring more skill in a relatively new medium.

Yet it seems to me that with "Photographic Studies" and "Studies from Life" Hawarden may also be drawing both playfully and seriously at once on the etymology and standard meanings of *study.* From the Latin *studium, study* means affection, devotion, partisan sympathy, desire, and pleasure. These usages, cited first in the OED with examples from Chaucer to Dryden, certainly apply to this mother-photographer's chosen subject matter and approach.

Equally important, and balancing the emotional connotations of the word, *study* also signifies a deliberate *mental* effort towards the accomplishment of a purpose. It thus denotes the acquisition of learning, the action of studying, even a room in a house used for private deliberations or reading and writing. In addition, *study* also is a synonym for mental preoccupations, abstractions, anxious thought, and reverie. Hawarden may herself be a student expending effort in her hobby, but the subject matter of her work surely involves her daughters as students of womanhood. Over and over in her sets, series, and pendants, Hawarden casts her children as students of life (in the theatrical and psychological sense of a quick or slow study) and, for their mother/photographer, they are studies from, in, and between phases and even decades of life. They study their mother and each other as models—whether turning inward or outward; hesitating on a threshold; playing out a courtship narrative in dress-up clothes; donning fluid gender roles with a change of costume, assuming male and female identities from ancient to modern times in varying skirts, pants, togas, undergarments, and overskirts; flirting, calmly looking at their reflection; lounging; or playing with each other's hair or fingers in studied attitudes of boredom, introspection, and desire. And she studies them in her studio, a room of her own, in which she can detect herself in them, and see them in her.

A telling photograph, in this studium/study/studio context, is that of daughter Isabella Grace clothed in a fashionable dark hat and dress

Figure 3. Lady Clementina Hawarden, "Clementina Maude,"
photographed at 5 Princes Gardens, South Kensington, London. About
1862–63; Albumen print from wet collodion negative. Victoria and Albert
Photography Department, London. Museum no. PH.457:344–1968.

of the 1860s, as if, Dodier suggests (1999, 41), she were going out in on a social call, dramatically paired with and contrasted to sister Florence Elizabeth, whose face is turned outward and whose dress and hat are light-colored and of another, earlier style. The photograph reads as if one daughter may represent her mother's girlhood, a stage with which she still identifies, while the other sister dresses like her mother the adult, but in her own maturing womanhood. Poignantly, the dark-dressed sister clothed in contemporary fashions looks back half-way at the house (and at us inside the house) that harbors her past, while the white-dressed sister in outdated fashions from the past looks beyond her sister into the distance and the future. Isabella's face is sharply delineated as she looks back; Florence's is blurred as she looks forward. Their half-embrace emblematizes a momentary meeting place of temporal and geographical horizons where identities mix, holding on to each other. Perhaps, too, this photograph best catches the maternally grasped, adolescent double moment of certainty/uncertainty. Poised at the epicenter of two vastly different worlds, a choice presents itself—which way to go, backward or forward?

While one could write a separate essay on those pictures involving role play and costumes, and yet another on those pairing models for a mirroring effect of same-sex desire, I want to focus here on three of the approximately one hundred photographs that employ the reflective glass of windows and mirrors. I shall treat this photographic trio as the thesis, antithesis, and synthesis of Hawarden's interests.[26]

In a well-known portrait from 1862–63, "Clementina Maude" stands full-figured clasping her hands together against the thin, light-colored curtains as if her sleeve or she herself were the cord holding them back (figure 3). She is bathed in natural light, and the lines of her right arm, her torso, her body, dress, and head are compositionally placed to reinforce patterns of light on the wall behind her and in the window frame, divided by the curtain. She is in a pose that can only be described as very difficult to hold, even pained. This print is a pendant to one in which the figure is positioned the same way, but reversed, turning to the left, inward, away from the window, with her hands clasped against the wall rather than the window curtain. For purposes of this argument, I am going to dwell on the first of the two, without losing sight that it is only one half of a pair.

Carol Mavor views coiled hair and clasped hands as images of frustration and confinement, invoking for comparison the Charlotte Perkins Gilman short story of desire, entrapment, and breakdown, "The Yellow Wallpaper." Mavor describes Hawarden's eldest daughter as a clipped angel of the house "pinned" to the wallpaper, marked by the shadows that mark the walls, and trapped at the window frame. In a similar vein, Dodier notes that the pose recalls for her the tortured position of the fallen woman in D. G. Rossetti's 1853 pen and ink *Found* and a clinging female in George Elgar Hicks's 1863 painting, *Woman's Mission: Companion to Manhood*.

Yet one might also note the arms that reach up towards the source of light and note that the coiled hair of the chignon is like a crown (is this figure a Ruskinian queen *and* a trapped angel?). For the young woman is as actively drawn to the light and the window as she may be hopelessly shut in by them, oppressed, or clinging—a point clearly illustrated by the pendant photograph. The dramatic pose struck there is one of prayer and even spiritual ecstasy. The light beams and lines of gauze curtains and their shadows form a triangle of striations—an inversion of beams such as that in Bernini's *The Ecstasy of St. Theresa*. Not necessarily a fallen woman or a trapped woman seeking escape from an oppressive interior, Clementina may also be like a butterfly moving towards the light, to an exterior positive world of sexual and/or spiritual fulfillment. Shadows of skirts and curtains, if one looks long enough, appear like wings.

Hawarden's daughters move back and forth across boundaries.[27] Many other prints—such as my second example, a photograph of Clementina standing in the window frame with an empty chair in the corner of the room—position the girls in between realms. Dressed in what appears to be an undergarment on top and an overskirt, with her back to the outside, it is not clear if she is going in or coming out. She emerges from the source of light and looks to be entering the domestic; yet it is equally possible that the empty Queen Anne-style chair, a common prop in the studio, represents her past, domestic childhood and not the empty seat waiting for the woman to fill it. Visual cues are ambiguous, and messages about her sexuality are conflicting. The blouse that slips off her shoulder does not help settle an interpretation—is she dressed as if she were in a state of disarray from a sexual encounter or pausing in the window before dressing for the day? Was there a ravishment and another figure who has departed? Or is the half-dressed girl testing the sunlight's warmth as she readies for the day, momentarily lost in a vacant reverie? Or is the photographer using her daughter as a sexually mature double of herself by looking back at the domestic interior of an earlier life, when a blouse hanging on a shoulder had nothing to do with heterosexual seduction?

I would argue not that the daughters are trapped, but that mother and daughters thrive in multiple relations to their inside and outside worlds, to domesticity, and to social requirements. The various sources of light both define and blur, create and dissolve physical materiality and suggest an alternative world touching on fairy tales or fantasies or dreams. This duality allows Hawarden to emphasize that perspective is not only Cartesian, in the sense of interior, introspective, privatized, and monocular, but fluid, simultaneously introspective and other-oriented, public and private, binocular and monocular, clear and blurry, defined and mysterious.

If the first photograph I discussed concerned a yearning towards light and ecstasy and the second pivoted on a movement back across the threshold into the domestic, the third offers a synthesis of those two impulses and yet remains equally dialectical itself by a simultaneous examination of both movements. Daughter Clementina looks at herself in a cheval mirror. Dressed in a dark hat and light-colored dress to go out, she examines her reflection. Though "something of a cliché" in portrait photography of the period (Dodier 1999, 41), the cheval mirror served Hawarden not as a comment on woman's vanity or to reflect a nude or to document a reflection, but to stress the differences between one view and another, one object and another. As Ramirez has noted, this type of photograph "fragmented and reorganized space while simultaneously offering two views of a sitter" (n.p., prefatory material): "By position-ing the cheval glass at certain angles, placing the figures in anomalous contingencies to the glass surface, and manipulating light and shadow, Hawarden was often able to create a reflection that was very different from its source and sometimes even completely obliterated" (Ramirez 61). Occupying the left half of the photograph, Clementina stands in profile and in front of a cheval glass that occupies the right half of the photograph. Her right hand holds her left wrist. Her left hand holds the stand of the mirror. What is blurring in the left portrait is clear in the reflection, and vice versa. Her face is clear in the left portrait and blurry in the glass. Her right sleeve is blurry in the left portrait and detailed in the mirror.

The profiled Clementina draws iconographically and composition-ally on a Renaissance profile tradition used for representations of aristo-crats and still common in nineteenth-century photographic images (see Wolf 176; Lalvani 448; Tagg 35). However, except for her use of classed clothing, Hawarden does not provide the props congruent with that tradition. Nor does she settle on a rigid profile, indicating "ornamental status" (Wolf 178).[28] Nor does Hawarden's placement of a dark hat on Clementina stress what a white dress alone might indicate: a figure of spiritual value or what a doubled white hat with dress might sug-gest—pure aesthetic dematerialization of form. The dark and light are provocatively mixed, as are the shadows and areas of focus. Like Ver-meer in *Woman with a Pearl Necklace*, Hawarden awards the woman the agency of viewing, thus making her a subject of self-absorption and not only an object of the observer's gaze. Unlike Vermeer's woman, she looks back seductively from the dark shadow of the mirror reflection at us.

Moreover, what she sees in the mirror is not just herself, but the very act of spectatorship. Clementina sees and is seen, thus recognizing, in Merleau-Ponty's words, "the 'other side'" of the "power of looking" (193) or the "reflexivity" of "the seeing-visible" (1964, 168). As Clementina sees herself seeing, we are aware of ourselves seeing her see herself and look back at us—we too are seeing, and seen, and called upon to be seen as photography and perception become the subject of the photograph.

By inviting the observer into this intersubjective and somatic relationship of seeing/being, Hawarden puts the viewer in a triple position. We are physically in the room seeing Clementina; we are outside the immediate visual space of the curve-topped mirror which we face, but in which we cannot literally see ourselves or a stand-in seeing (as in, say, Las Meninas), and lastly, we remain outside, standing back, seeing the two almost equal halves–being and reflection—as if they were parts of a linked but not fully joined heart.

Clementina's fully embodied action of looking occurs partly in darkness, like the photographer's face and cloth, and partly in light, like the eye of the lens. Is the hat, sign of social calls and of going out into the public world as a woman, the daughter's own or does it belong to her mother? Is this a dress rehearsal for growing up or the real thing? Looking forward to adulthood in the mirror, Clementina's face in the mirror is darkened and blurred; yet looking from the mirror back into the childhood world, a woman sees her childhood past as clear and vivid. As her future looks back at her, her reflection also is looking at the present as past.

This stereoscopic image in one frame fully destroys monocularism, as Clementina looks out and back at once and faces different ways due to the angle of the mirror. She puts "vision into the visible" (Prendeville, on Merleau-Ponty 377). The pose is erotically charged because of the mirror frame and the position of her hands, indicating that entering the public world also means entering adult sexuality. Holding onto the leg of the cheval frame, Clementina holds that arm back at the wrist, and still. It is a half-gesture. With her left hand positioned—and reflected to make a pair in the form of a benediction—and her right hand positioned and reflected to make a second pair as reaching out and holding onto the mirror, Clementina remains divided. Her attitudes don't speak the same coding. Shadows and the wooden mirror leg divide them, making the touching of the mirror the marker of a transition from girlhood to womanhood.

As Craig Owens indicates, in her photographs with mirrors, Hawarden consciously or unconsciously explores "the structural tension within the medium—between photography as extrovert, a view on the material world, and the photograph as a self-enclosed image of its own process" (80). Although he does not say so, Hawarden sees that structural tension manifested daily in her daughters' social roles and their girlhood reveries and in her own psychosocial experience of seeing/experiencing/mothering girls becoming women.

Because of their repetitive focus on the body and its relation to light and place, Hawarden's photographs draw on an embodied perception in the observer, involving more than a simply specular view. Hawarden's photographs invite the observer to a synesthetic visual experience that is not a purely mental construct, not textual, but visceral first and only then processed mentally as emblematic of temporal processes of change at the site of female identity. She especially appeals to women viewers but asks us all to consider how we are ourselves placed in the world and to reconsider the experience of our corporeality, our being in the world (Merleau-Ponty 1964, 133–43; Bal 2003, 14). Her photographs question how we perform acts of seeing others, while she emphasizes, repeatedly and intentionally, a kind of late-Turner vanishing point—dissolution into shadow or light, not disappearance into the distance. I would go further to argue that the enlargement of the visual experience Hawarden demands, the thinking of sensation and the eroticism of thought, is also a dialectical one—mental to visceral—in which each continually redefines the other.

In experimenting with sources of light, windows, glass, frames, sills, and mirrors, Hawarden illustrates that vantage points are not always clear and that our view of figures and the meanings we attach to them can never be monocular, singular, or fixed. The eye is part of the body, not to be trusted entirely in a world of diffuse light, encroaching shadows, doubling, and reduplications—sometimes not to be trusted at all. Yet, in asserting that there is no unchanging real objective reality but only a changing one, she does not reduce meaning to aestheticism, to moods, to the sublime, to the symbolic, to the transcendent, or to enigma. Rather she explores and even celebrates transparent and reflective layers of experience, showing how in one framed view, one photograph, an observer may jostle against and within various and divergent vistas, temporal moments, and felt spaces.

Hawarden here begins to do with light, shadow, and mirror what Whistler took up differently in his *Woman in White* series and what Pablo Picasso fully exploited later in developing cubism, when he used a broken camera lens and prism to show how light, angle, and mirrors can condition what and how we see.[29] Like Turner, Hawarden demonstrates that empirical experience is far more provisional than we think. That she does so with photography in the early 1860s is unusual. In single shot after single shot and in two major exhibition groupings, she exposes the Cartesian perspective model as insufficiently embodied, neither physiological enough nor complicated enough to capture "life."

CHAPTER FOUR

Points of View in "Pippa Passes," *The Woman in White,* and *Silas Marner*

point of view n. [after French point de vue *(1689; earlier in technical senses: see point of sight n.]; the position from which something is seen or viewed; (fig.) the perspective from which a subject or event is perceived, or a story, etc., narrated; a mental position or attitude (now the usual sense).*

—*OED online*

The narrating agent of a text and its "point of view" are not the same. Agency raises the question of who supplies the narration, while point of view raises the question of whose vision determines what is being narrated.

—*Steven Cohan and Linda M. Shires 94*

GEOMETRIC PERSPECTIVE AND POINT OF VIEW

What does visual perspective have to do with narrative point of view? Can one really talk in the same breath about painting, photography, fiction, and poetry despite real generic differences? Critics such as Mieke Bal, whose work bridges visual studies and narratology, maintain that the objective point of view of realism in literature is closest to Renaissance perspective in the visual arts. Like Renaissance geometric perspective, realism assumes a mastering point of view through an external, invisible third-person narrator–focalizer who offers an authoritative, often omniscient view of characters and events.[1] Literary realism, as is well known, thus proposes a certain kind of subject, knowledge of objective facts, and a one-way relationship with the object. By drawing attention to the "reality effect" (Barthes 12) of that which is represented, realism enforces dominant ideological claims. It seems to do so from a single position in space and time through false neutrality, as if the narrator said: "Look, this is real!" In other words, like Renaissance perspective, it does so without exploring the construction of its position and its claim to know—it appears neutral.

During the nineteenth century, narrative literary texts demonstrate increasingly complicated techniques of narration and focalization as they question omniscient authority and the providential plot. Some time ago, J. Hillis Miller argued that narrative omniscience located its authority in the decline of religious belief in Victorian culture. The authority of the narrator in Victorian fiction, he argued, is a way to believe in something or someone who appears secure, rather than slipping into relativism (1968, 30).[2] This strikes me as an important part of a larger explanation. Many poets and novelists remain skeptical about establishing an objective point of view, as they respond to the reorganization and increasing psychologization of vision. They translate a seemingly godlike, stable vision into points of view. Moreover, the narrative's narrator is not always the focalizer. For, with a new stress on hermeneutics, alterations in kinds of legal testimony and evidence, and new advances in science, as well as a changing relationship between literary texts and biblical authority, literary forms increasingly and self-consciously stage questions about meaning and interpretation through point of view.[3] Though tamed by reading practices that stressed a narrative hermeneutic and that were themselves influenced by a teleological pacing often facilitated by serialization, numerous novels and poems ironize or otherwise revise both the subjectivity of a Romantic "I" as well as the neutrality of an "objective" point of view. They spread out perspective into a prism-like panoply of perspectives on an object that is itself changeful.

This chapter will take up two novels from 1859 to 1861, in light of the poetry of Robert Browning. I will enlist Browning's "Pippa Passes" to show how George Eliot's *Silas Marner* and Wilkie Collins's *The Woman and White* introduce spatially and temporally complex perspectives that rely on multiple standpoints. In considering poetry and fiction in light of the visual arts and photography, I depart from prior criticism.[4] Because these texts foreground perspective and point of view as mental conditions and as social constructs—and thus as a political as well as a formal problem—Browning, Collins, and Eliot challenge our thinking about narrative, time, and space and take narrative in new directions.

Discourses such as neuroscience, mesmerism, trance, or depth psychology, infiltrating verbal constructs, altered forms as well as content (see Winter). Thus, for instance, when Wilkie Collins's novels move beyond the older epistolary forms based on social performance, they edge towards legal case discourse and individual statements. Witnesses, documents, and fragmentary memories are brought to bear by a central but fallible 'collector–narrator' on a set of questions or issues. Jenny Bourne Taylor suggests that Collins's "stories involve not only complex explorations of forms of perception, of consciousness, and cognition, but also . . . the shaping of social identity" (1). Collins's formal experimentation with point of view strikes me as symptomatic of the more far-reaching cultural pattern I have been describing. From the 1830s and 1840s, Tennyson, Barrett, and Browning had already experimented with alternative modes of perception, consciousness, and cognition, as they mounted critiques of a number of institutions (slavery, female education, patriarchy, the domestic) and cultural practices (the cult of the child, gender double standards, hero worship). They contributed to an increasing cultural psychologization of vision by foregrounding perception through their handling and development of point of view.

It hardly seems surprising, therefore, that Nicholas Dames, a scholar of the novel, finds that nineteenth-century critics treated the form of the novel as a temporal process and not as an object (209). Nor is it surprising that he should view the novel as an experience of "oscillation between 'relaxing' subplots . . . and the more rigidly hermeneutic drives of suspense and revelation" (214).[5] Dames accepts teleology–the hallmark of the novel reading process—as necessary, but also at some odds with the spatial and temporal complexities of reading demanded by the actual Victorian novel's form(s).

The double poem that challenged the fixity of "type" (i.e., "fixed categories of thought and language ordained by God which governed relationships") came to signify a "nonteleological" order of experience (I. Armstrong 1993, 16) that affected other literary constructions. Still, as Dames suggests, the teleological drive of narrative seems to have blunted our appreciation of the self-questioning and hyperconsciousness of nineteenth-century prose fiction almost as much as the prevalence of critical habits that continue to cling to outmoded notions of realism and to stress symmetry, unity, or mastery of point of view.[6] A self-consciousness about representation and point of view clearly links early Victorian texts as disparate in form or politics as Alfred Tennyson's "Mariana" (1830) and "The Lady of Shalott" (1832) or Charles Dickens's string of social observations, "Sketches by Boz" (1836). It seems fruitful, therefore, to reconsider nineteenth-century fiction and poetry as being in conversation with each other and with a visual art that had challenged the perspectival paradigm offering new models for seeing. Within a literature of heightened self-consciousness about representation, then, a mobile observer, moving pictures, shifts of perspective, and even breaks in temporal sequence offered early- and mid-nineteenth-century writers an analogous testing ground for questioning a single, mastering perspective.

Like challenges to Renaissance perspective that painting, poetry, the prose essay, and photography mounted, which I analyzed in previous chapters, fiction subverted the omniscience of a central authoritative point of view in various ways. Nineteenth-century literary texts specifically focus on the relationship of the reader to a guiding narrator or lyric speaker, a relationship exposed as partial and insufficient. It is, therefore, hardly a coincidence that the case specimen study—that prime legal, medical, and scientific locus which the Enlightenment had employed— should be taken up as a renewed staple of poetic and narrative form by Victorian poets and novelists who now placed an emphasis on process, even a bringing to trial—rather than on precedent or example.[7]

The three salient texts that this chapter will examine, however, deploy the case study not merely to examine the object under scrutiny, but also to undermine the very possibility of a unidirectional gaze or a neutral gaze on a single object, whether by character or narrator or reader. These texts still retain the sympathetic identification that separates nineteenth-century literature from Modernist texts. Yet that sympathy cannot be established without the reader's struggle with a burden of perception, identification, and understanding. For the nineteenth-century poets and novelists who draw on literary/legal/scientific constructs to frame a relation of subject to object inevitably create a dialogic relationship of objectivity and subjectivity. They test a reader by persistently throwing off a consistent or single point of view. They redefine truth by inquiring into self-illusions and cultural fictions, and by implicating consciousness in dubious projections and questionable cultural categories. In other words, like the double poem, the case study as used in the nineteenth century stresses epistemology rather than ontology both internally (character to character, narrator to character, narrator to itself) as well as externally (reader to character, reader to narrator or speaker).

As a chief mode of literary discourse in the period, the case study thus illustrates the failures of scientific rigor or an ideal objectivity precisely because the subjectivity of the gazer, whether omniscient third person or limited first person, is itself on display for investigation. As Mieke Bal puts it: "the objective third person, the Cartesian cogito sustaining classical perspective and its relationship to the 'real' is bound up with subjectivity as much as with objectivity, with closeness as much as distance—it is, in Philippe Lejeune's apt phrase: 'autobiography in the third person'" (1996, and quoting Lejeune 170–71). If the Victorians themselves did not clearly articulate this point, they certainly demonstrated its force in their investigation of narrative point of view, whether through multiple narrators in *Wuthering Heights*, through a deceptive narrator in *Villette*, through an ironic narrator in *Vanity Fair*, through dual narration of omniscience and first person as in *Bleak House*, or through a dramatic case frame as in *Heart of Darkness*. Readers of nineteenth-century texts are plunged into examinations of lives, kinds of evidence, and points of view.

In a recent essay on the case, the sentimental novel, and *Lord Jim* (1901), James Chandler offers a genealogy of the literary case study useful to this chapter. He argues for permutations from the 1750s to the 1900s, but he only briefly treats the Victorian period, moving on to innovative uses of point of view in "modern fiction" (864).[8] Chandler rightly argues for the changing nature of the case as "a discourse, genre and way of thinking" (837) in fiction since that of Daniel Defoe. Between the "early adaptation of the judgment form of the case from ethics and law and the later adaptation of the individuation form of the case from medicine and science," he suggests, there is "a lesser known, intermediate moment in the history of the case—the sentimental form" (837). This moment he locates in the 1750s when the word *sentimental* begins to be associated with "a new way of producing narrative" (840). Though he might have turned to David Hume or Edmund Burke (see Wahrman 187), Chandler cites Adam Smith's very famous theory of an anticasuistical, mobile, moral sympathy (i.e., fellow-feeling) as central to the case study model. He links it directly, as others have done, to the theory and practice of point of view, essential to the novel form: "whether or not it is cast in quasi-theological terms," he says, "the notion of sentimental mobility ramifies through the subsequent history of fiction in the theory and practice of point of view."[9] He largely bypasses nineteenth-century literature, as his aim is to demonstrate, with great care, how Joseph Conrad's 1901 novel, structured by a sentimental case framework, mixes modalities of case logic: the ethical/legal and the medical/psychological with structures of observation and narration that range across various points of view.

Robert Browning's "Pippa Passes" (1841), Wilkie Collins's *The Woman in White* (1859–60), and George Eliot's *Silas Marner* (1861) challenge classical single-point perspective through case studies which feature issues of vision and consciousness in the diegesis (the telling of events as narrative), while foregrounding point of view, including vision and consciousness, as a problem on the levels of narration, focalization, and structure.[10] My three examples not only range over a quarter of a century, but they also represent three of the most important genres of the period, lyric drama, sensation fiction, and classic realism, and thus serve as indices to a larger problematic in literary culture. Although quite different from each other in many respects, they are representative of different ways writers increasingly struggled with perspective, godlike omniscience, and complicated questions of vision and knowledge. Browning's poetic drama stages the journey of an unconscious, innocent girl of faith through a worldly town among people who plot against each other and against her; Wilkie Collins's novel promotes subjective first-person fact finding in the figure of Walter Hartright over a more distant and objectively based legal case, yet also reveals the mix of sensation with reason in all testimony; George Eliot's fiction counterpoints—within third-person narration with occasional forays into first person—stories of a trusting weaver afflicted with catalepsy and the morally bankrupt who steal from him when he is blind and unconscious. All concern cases—cases of individual lives in strange situations; cases of murder, theft, and loss; case situations in which the reader is implicated; cases the narrator investigates. Each explores the relationship of seeing to consciousness. In each, readers face what counts as a case—what kind of people have become exemplary of what—who counts as an expert? Are sympathy and identification possible, whether on the part of a narrator, narrator-character, or a reader, and to what degree?[11] Each reinforces such a quest by using dialogism on varied narrative levels—Browning through an ironic and a dramatic structure; Collins through juxtaposition of points of view which themselves must be questioned and by consistently drawing attention to testimony as fiction and the novel as representation; Eliot through an exquisitely linked double plot and with a self-reflexive narrative voice.

In the replacement of godlike authority with a standard of ethics based in sympathy and judgment, these nineteenth-century writers experiment with form and narration. Replacing any direct, overriding moral compact such as that which Chandler still finds in the eighteenth century, they wrangle with varying modes of belief. Their emphasis on untrustworthiness of vision and their demystification of single consciousness leads their reader to rely less on the neutral position of moral sympathetic identification and judgment promoted by Adam Smith, than on a continuing analytic struggle with competitive meanings and multiple layers of representation.

Since the eighteenth century, narratives had relied on case studies to examine particular and individual fates. Yet even writers who believed in a divine order were increasingly hard pressed to assert a convincing argument for an overriding theological design. Ambivalent about religion, the young Robert Browning takes up such a problem in "Pippa Passes" by positing the case of an innocent who strongly believes in God's design but who moves through a fallen world.

WINDOWS ON PIPPA'S PASSAGE

"Pippa Passes" was published as the first volume of Robert Browning's *Bells and Pomegranates* in 1841. Subtitled "A Drama," it is read as a closet drama, rather than one to be acted on the stage. In Browning's original plan, the poem was to become part of an ambitious hybrid project involving lyric, prose, blank verse, and drama. He stages the scene in a high Italian hilltop town, yet beneath framed windows to explore perspectivalism. As lyric speaker, the innocent Asolo factory girl Pippa, on her one holiday of the year, plays a game of impersonation by trying to imagine herself in the position of those she considers the "Happiest Four" inhabitants of her town. "For am I not this day, whate'er I please?" (Part I. ll.104–5). Yet her act of desire and fellow-feeling is ironized as false projection. It is the reader, not Pippa, who observes and sees the four for what they truly are. And that reader must sympathize with but analytically distance herself from the romantic naïf who wishes that she were as loved and cherished as she believes her visual objects to be.

Playing out her "fancy's fullest games" (Part I. l.110), Pippa desires to put herself in the position of one who is truly loved. "Someone shall love me, as the world calls love; I am no less than Ottima, take warning!" (Part I. ll.115–16). Yet Pippa falsely views each of the "Happiest Four" as better than the last. Indeed, the poetic sequence of scenes glimpsed through windows as Pippa walks along presents a seeming hierarchy from carnal love (Scene 1.119–20: Ottima is passionately loved by Sebald), conjugal love (1.130: Phene is romantically loved by Jules), parental love (1.164: Luigi is unconditionally loved by his mother), and love of God (1.180–82: the Monsignor is loved by his God). Through dramatic irony, the nature of the characters and the dramatic actions going on behind the windows are revealed to the reader, but not to Pippa, who literally spends the day walking by their abodes. As the reader comes to understand, the figures whom Pippa considers to be fulfilled and worthy of love are either perpetrating a crime or have been tricked into deceptions by others. Thus Pippa never is privy to the revelation of a murder by Sebald of Ottima's husband Luca or to the likelihood of their double suicide. Nor does she know that the artist Jules has been tricked into marriage to Phene, a model; that an anarchist intends to murder the Austrian emperor; or that she herself is the object of a plot that only the Monsignor can abort at the eleventh hour. Love is hardly secure in the world of Asolo; rather it is being tested, refused, questioned, and betrayed.

As Pippa passes beside and beneath their various house and turret windows, she sings lyrical songs such as the most famous which ends "God's in his heaven—All's right with the world!" (Part I. ll.227–28). Heard by these "worthies" at moral turning points, the lyrics may, or may not, affect their character transformation. I will return to this critically debated point about Pippa's influence. Still, however critics may judge her possible influence, they all agree that this "little ragged girl" (Part I. l.230) and impressionistic naïf, through her misguided projections, superimposes a purity that cannot be extracted from the corrupt world through which she walks. At the same time, framed by Browning as an artist figure, she survives remarkably immune. She walks through a snake pit unaware that she may be bitten at any moment.

This poem is as fascinating for its setting and situation as for its content and ethics. Throughout the poem, Browning plays with Leon Battista Alberti's *De Pictura,* the classic fifteenth-century Italian treatise on perspective that first used the window as a metaphor to explain how we view a pictorial image through a frame in perspective.[12] Taking an immobile viewer as the central point, Alberti had instructed artists to treat the painting's frame as an open-window view on the object. Browning subtly reconfigures Alberti's Renaissance model for the space of vision by using the window motif in several antithetical ways. When he frames views that are far different from those Pippa imagines, Browning drives a wedge between imaginative sympathy and brutal reality. This has the effect of questioning the identificatory processes of innocent looking and fellow feeling, even while it opens the lives of the worthies for inspection. It exposes Pippa as blind and unperceptive, if moral. What Pippa has seen in the past in her town of the worthies is irrelevant; what she knows in the present is equally irrelevant, except as it reveals more about her than about the objects of her sight or knowledge. It is, in fact, through her blindness that the reader sees, as her innocence defamiliarizes the worthiness of the "Happy Four."

The irony of this drama of consciousness is heightened by the subject matter and lyricism of Pippa's songs concerning God, the grace of Kings, or love. For her songs' tone and meanings are understood by the reader as being entirely disconnected in assumptions and intentions from the actions and lives on the other side of the windows. Complicating further the literal and figurative notions of transparency, Browning's text also suggests that for those inside, such as the vain Ottima, the window frame may be a mirror, not a window at all: "This dusty pane might serve for a looking glass" (1.121), she cries while isolating a few gray hairs. Thus Browning introduces a visual system and an epistemology that, unlike a window, refuses the mediation of inside and outside. The pane of glass serves itself to mirror a fallen world, self-interest, and a blockage of vision—indicating that those behind the windows may be so consumed by surfaces and self-constructions that they are fundamentally untouched by anything external to them, and certainly incapable of a reciprocal sympathy. By extension, the presence of the mirror serves as a commentary on Pippa. The looking glass illuminates epistemology in the poem, making the reader wonder about all the frames: do we see what we think and want to see? Do we see what we view or ourselves in a frame? How does a frame shape but also limit a view or an observation? Browning explores the psychologism of vision on all sides.

"Pippa Passes" also redefines Alberti's window frame motif for perspective, based in Cartesian subjectivity, by providing a mobile Pippa, not an immobile gazer. Pippa's mobility and her relationship to the window frames she passes, presumably not frontally, but sideways, call into question the representational system and scopic regime of the fixed position of viewing. In "Pippa Passes" Browning moves away from a Romantic treatment of a lyrical point of view in which a conscious subject or an "I" assumes a view on an object rendered as a he, a she, or an it. Rather than making Pippa an omniscient seer who knows others and herself, but is herself unknown, Browning ironizes her as elect, but unseeing and unknowing. She never enters any other point of view. As E. Warwick Slinn puts it, she passes by, but she does not pass into the lives of others.[13] In flipping perception and perceived, Browning questions the exemplarity of Pippa, turning the view onto the reader, whom he tests.

In stressing different scenes and people in the acts of the drama, rather than a clear, developing cause-and-effect plot, Browning also reshapes the notion of a journey. To be sure, Browning segments his drama into four sequential acts: Morning, Noon, Evening, Night, but he does not relate the scenes. Nor are the four acts and multiple perspectives unified by the sun, nor are they united by Pippa's passage or songs. In fact, despite the motif of the linear journey through space, the Cartesian coordinate system of space is altered here to a series of parallel universes (houses) that the reader experiences as juxtaposed in a montage construct. As the reader moves through the scenes, he continually shifts the center—and thus the focus—of the reading experience, reentering in different places to adopt a provisional point of view. This multiple window entry into the poem itself gives the impression that the innocent journey through a corrupt, fallen world is not a position of absolute knowledge or truth, but rather a contingent, historical construction.

While other critics have commented on tonal differences from section to section, it is worth noting that each part of the poem is written in a different literary style: melodrama, romance, political drama, and Jacobean drama of intrigue. The text thus draws attention to the fictiveness of poetic style—writing's historicity—even to its status as representation through reference to paper and ink (II. Interlude after ll.325ff). In so doing, Browning toys again with Aristotelian dramatic unity, thus further shattering the Alberti frame. By spatializing time, foregrounding representation, and leaving plot issues unresolved, his text moves both lyric and drama into new directions for the nineteenth century, directions which he would extend in subsequent dramatic monologues. The fact that these formal issues are also defining features of Modernism, by traditional accounts, illustrates how far the twentieth century went in reading the nineteenth century as tame and boring.

"Pippa Passes" illustrates perspective to be an effect of narrative as it is read, rather than an authoritative unifying device; the reader approaches through different windows, not through a single or simple orienting path to knowledge. Browning uses Pippa's passing "under the window" (1.296) to explore the limits of a single point of view, the power (or not) of a moral lyric to move an audience, and to illustrate an array of perspectives. Browning seems to suggest that locating truth, understanding situations, and making an ethical judgment all demand struggle and negotiation, not adherence to a fixed, predetermined point of view.

Combining teleology and randomness by setting a providential plot in a highly self-conscious picaresque structure, Browning's text actually mocks the sentimental journey of the eighteenth century that Chandler notes as a defining modality of nineteenth-century case logic, while acknowledging but still questioning a teleological and a theological foundation for meaning. Immune to a world of fortuitousness and

piously believing in a world ordained by Divine Benevolence, "All service ranks the same with God" (Part IV. l.113), Pippa walks through an
order that is shattered, fragmented, and confused.

In exposing an unchecked, wishful sympathy, Browning further
exploits contingency. The fact that Pippa walks by particular homes and
conversations at critical moments shows the power of chance in producing truth for the reader, if not for Pippa. Finally, there is a layering of
events and of temporal modes of inside/outside (events inside rooms/
outside under windows) and of inner time/exterior time (consciousness
including memory/acts). The relationship between these layers is one of
asymmetry. If we think of Pippa's walk and songs as the literally exterior
events—of location and action—the turning points and the conclusion of
the plot do not rest in those events, but in the interior ones, both mental
and physical. Instead of inner character processes motivating and driving the plot, as would be traditional in a realist construct, the contingent
exterior events and time frame (Pippa's walk) are juxtaposed to a succession of powerful interior events and processes among characters (behind
windows) and to psychological events and processes undertaken by a
tested reader (among the lines on the page).

I mentioned that I would return to the critical debate about Pippa's
influence on those she passes. Some critics argue that Pippa's songs
lead to characters' moral transformation (see Fish 846; Garrett 47–49;
Korg 5; Hair 52), while others argue for uncertainty and Pippa's lack of
influence (King 48; Kramer 241–49; Slinn 1976, 158–59), and still others
seem to keep the equivocation of the poem intact (Tucker 1980, 124).
My close reading of the poem's language indicates that there is ambiguity surrounding events, time, place, and eventualities: it is unclear
if Ottima and Sebald commit suicide, if both do, or in what order; it is
not sure when or if Jules and Phene wed, since they simply exit; it is
not known if Luigi fulfills his assassination attempt, because we can't
know what he means with "'Tis God's voice calls; how can I stay?" and
finally it is unclear if Pippa, a secret heiress, will inherit rightfully or be
killed, though it does seem that the Monsignor, implicated in the plot,
feels guilty, because he apparently asks for forgiveness: "Miserere mei,
Domine!" (IV before Pippa's final scene).

Yet despite all the uncertainty, because Pippa believes in God and
because she is representative of a divine order and innocence and may
emerge unharmed, despite threats on her life, the poem retains some of
the optimism and the feeling of moral transformation that its very ambiguity and multiplicity deny. The same complexity is located in its title: to
pass means an act of passage, departure from life, a course of action, to

happen, to seem to be someone else, to desist or refuse, to satisfy those who examine one, to bring to completion, and a sleight of hand trick, as in changing position in a card game. All of these meanings are in play in this lyrical drama.

Like the later "My Last Duchess," a monologue delivered and heard before an affixed painting, "Pippa Passes" explores the fluid relationship of truth and reality by denying the authority of a framed view. By stressing a picaresque mode of random occurrence, "Pippa Passes" attempts to plumb experience—to go deeper into the everyday—to see all sides, to peek around the corner of the view limited by traditional Renaissance, classical perspective, both at the "I" inscribed in that viewing and at the multiple dimensions of the seemingly static objects in the view. "Pippa Passes" not only emblematizes the relationship between single perspective and multiple shifting positions, but also that between one point of view about self and another point of view. The poem can thus be seen as a dramatic working out of the relationship between a viewing position and positions of interpretation.

Years later, when Browning returned to similar issues on a larger scale in the highly popular *The Ring and the Book* (1868–69), he more explicitly showed vision as an unreliable guide to truth and more programmatically exposed language as subject to distortions. Yet drawing on legal evidence in a trial as his model for the case there, he also indicated, again through irony, that a reader sifting through various tellings about one set of events might, finally, gain fragments of truth. In his early statement of similar issues, "Pippa Passes," Browning dramatizes how the very process of weighing points of view, setting one against another or in layers spatially in the reader's mind, undoes a temporal unfolding via a sentimental journey that ostensibly leads to a truth. The truth of an event, the poem indicates, is not possible to discover through either a framed view or through teleology.

"VAST PERSPECTIVES OF SUCCESS UNROLL THEMSELVES BEFORE MY EYES" (FOSCO)

In his fifth novel, *The Woman in White* (1859–60), Wilkie Collins extended the narrative experimentation that he had employed in earlier fictions such as *Basil* (1852) by further moving the English novel towards a reliance on individual consciousness. Yet that consciousness is open to interrogation. While *Basil* had deftly structured the narrative in terms of a confession, a diary, and letters, Collins's later novel, a mystery, plays even more overtly with point of view, by fragmenting into multiple testimonies an older epistolary mode invested in consensus.[14] Collins seems to endorse individual point of view, even that of a written object such as a tombstone, as important to investigations.

All points of view are not, however, equal in their perspective on reality, he shows, and some valuable ones are erased or entirely omitted. The subtitle chosen above, "Vast perspectives of success unroll themselves before my eyes," is written by the book's villain Count Fosco at the end of a "postscript" he willfully adds to Marian Halcombe's diary (359) while she is unconscious. He literally overwrites her point of view with his own, taking the space of her private diary to do so. While rightly often interpreted in terms of gender politics, this moment is also highly significant as emblematic of the trials of point of view. At first glance, the narrative seems to be all about attaining the right perspective to get at the truth of a mystery of identity, whether that perspective be physical, visual, or aural (Marian Halcombe's climbing on a roof to get a better view), verbal and mental (a testimony about a death), or emotional (Walter's devotion to Laura is single minded). Yet, as we come to see, it is difficult to maintain point of view in the novel, and for some, notably Laura and Anne, narrating one's point of view does not ever occur. Ultimately this novel signals not just the splitting of narrative point of view into numerous perspectives, but the exposure of truth telling as falsehood and the affirmation of the real as a mystery.[15]

Begun as a serial in 1859 for Dickens's journal *All the Year Round* to sustain the involvement the serialization of *A Tale of Two Cities* had created, *The Woman in White* more than fulfilled its aim. A best-seller, the novel sold more copies of the journal than had Dickens's exciting French Revolution narrative, went through seven editions in six months, and inspired the manufacture of 'woman in white' cloaks, bonnets, and music (Lonoff 72). Its influence continued; a large advertising poster has been credited with inaugurating a new phase in poster art. It has been linked to the paintings of Whistler. It has generated at least eight film or television versions and in 2004 was the basis for the Andrew Lloyd Webber musical.

Yet, well beyond the suspense generated by the mystery of stolen female identity and the excitement generated by a ruthless yet tender foreign villain, the novel holds the reader because of its unconventional narrative techniques. As many literary critics note, the novel registers a conflicted relationship to realism and its dominant ideologies. Critics have disagreed, however, over whether Collins's handling of realism is based in challenge (Hughes; J. Taylor; Heller), subversion (Knoepfl-macher 1975), conservative reinforcement (Cvetkovich), or if his text is symptomatic of a breach with realism (Kendrick) or registers a crisis within realism (Brantlinger). Alternatively, it is considered analogous to realism in its sharing of duplicity and its fascination with lies as well as truth telling (Kucich).[16] My focus lies on what the form of this novel enacts and what it tells us about perspective.

In his 1860 Preface to the three-volume edition, Collins explains that he devised a formal "experiment" with narrative point of view: "The story of the book is told throughout by the characters of the book. They are all placed in different positions along the chain of events; and they all take the chain up in turn, and carry it on to the end" (Collins 1860; Bachman and Cox 618). With this statement, Collins challenges the way the novel is understood during the period as one of character or of plot. While critics have established the sensation novel as a fiction of 'event,' not of character development, the titillation of sensation fiction always emerges from the overt disjunction between the story and its tellings. It is a fiction of and about partial perspectives and the dialogue generated among and between them.

The Preamble, which I take to be written by Walter Hartright, a paint-ing teacher who teaches landscape painting and classical perspective, likens the novel to depositions made by witnesses in a law case.[17] The Preamble writer thus appears, in one guise, as a collector and editor of evidence. "He seems to be replacing divine judgment with empirical evidence that emerges as both reliable and relative" (J. Taylor 110). The evidence is reliable, it seems, because it is founded in experience and edited out of good intentions. Yet it is relative precisely because it is founded in experience and because the motives involved are not neces-sarily all honorable. Thus the initial perspective presented to the reader is, in the end, shown to be limited and questionable. For, as the narrative proceeds, we see that Hartright's bias is borne of romantic involvement with Laura Fairlie. Still later, by fathering the son who transgresses class boundaries to become the heir of Limmeridge, Walter Hartright's new class vantage point raises the issue of motives for his fascination with Laura and for telling this story that may or may not include love. In this case, the retrospective selection and editing could be read as a lower-middle-class outsider's justification of property acquisition, as much as a palimpsest of informed points of view collected out of devotion to solve the mystery about someone else's stolen identity and spent dowry.

The reader's role as a weigher of different points of view is thus established immediately, even though we are not sure that this is retrospectively told by a character. For we read that this is a case not tried in court but presented through similar testimonies. A formal presentation was out of the question, according to the teller, because the "[l]aw is still, in certain inevitable cases, the pre-engaged servant of the long purse" (33). It is well known that Collins had studied the law and that he had had investigated particular French trials before penning *The Woman in White*. In an old book stall in Paris, he located an account of trials much like those in the English Newgate Calendar. From these emerged the plot for his novel: the substitution of one girl for another and a burial. In the Preface to the French edition of the novel (1861), Collins explains how he came up with the idea for telling the story through many narrative points of view after listening to trial proceedings: "As each one rose to provide his portion of personal involvement and as, from one end of the investigation to the other each separate link was connected to the others to form an incontrovertible chain of evidence, I felt that my attention was being increasingly ensnared." Collins goes on to describe how a fiction based on such a succession of individual testimonies could "slip into the mind of the reader this conviction, this faith" (621). The Preamble declares that to get at the truth each character will tell those portions of the narrative for which he or she is responsible. The objective is "to present the truth always in its most direct and most intelligible aspect" (33). If Hartright is to pose as a defense attorney, the other characters, both major and minor, are to act as witnesses and the reader to become the judge and jury of a narrative conducted as a trial.

The analogy of this fiction to a trial is, however, knowingly specious. Just as Browning questioned projection and belief and Eliot will explore the limits of perception and sympathy, Collins explores the ethics and legitimacy of case study itself. In a trial the judge and jury know from the start why witnesses are being presented, what the case to be judged is about, the nature of the crime and charges. They are present to weigh facts in as objective a manner as possible. This is not so in *The Woman in White*. In fact, we have no idea that the narratives of Hartright, Gilmore, Marian Halcombe, Frederick Fairlie, or Mrs. Michaelson—the narratives of the first part—are introduced as part of a "case" to reinstate the identity of Laura Fairlie, Lady Glyde. It is not until the end of the first part, in fact, when sixty percent of the novel is over, that we discover Laura is presumed to be dead. More chapters go by before we discover what happened to her and that Hartright is collecting scraps of evidence, the depositions we read, against some later presentation of them all. Ironically, Laura will be reawarded her identity only after male villagers and estate workers have voiced their *opinions*, after viewing her, that she is

Laura. She has come to look so much like Anne Catherick, however, due to her suffering, that the reader-as-judge cannot be absolutely positive of the verdict.

Deprived of foresight, and skeptical about sureties, the reader of *The Woman in White* who is left in the same time scheme as the characters is thus forced to share their uncertainty. The narrative chronology is cast as a reconstruction—Gilmore's narration, for example, is written after Laura has been maltreated by Sir Percival Glyde, after she has been presumed dead and resurrected, and long after Glyde is removed. The equation of truth at a trial and truth created by narratives in a fiction, so strongly asserted by the Preamble, then, is a ruse. In fact, Collins insists that our own subjectivities are so involved—our own sensations are so "touched"—that suspense prevents knowing or judging.

The character of the contemporary reception of the *Woman in White* illustrated a short circuit among affect, reason, and judgment. As Alison Winter has outlined, readers did not use the moral sciences to describe their experience of reading this book. "Here the route from page to nerve was direct" rather than mediated (323). Mrs. Oliphant in *Blackwoods* offered the most informative response about the thrilling spell of *The Woman in White* on a reader, describing a physical, physiological set of effects that powerfully drove out reason or self-conscious thought in a way unprecedented in reader response previously, even with Dickens. Collins's claim that the book was an experiment in narrative point of view, suggests Winter, might be secondary to the experiment in mesmerizing his readers; yet I think these go hand in hand.

Like both Browning and George Eliot, Collins questions omniscience and the providential plot.[18] Handling his chief narrator with some self-reflexive play, Collins literalizes the metaphor of the author(ity) as artist in the figure of Walter Hartright.[19] And Hartright's deficiencies are evident from the start as his vision immediately gets compromised by his nerves; he is confused by the object viewed and is hampered by his methods of viewing. A reader's uneasiness about Hartright's credentials intensify as soon as he attempts to interpret the woman in white, Anne Catherick. "What sort of a woman she was, and how she came to be out alone in the high-road, an hour after midnight, I altogether failed to guess. . . . It was like a dream. Was I Walter Hartright?" (56–57). Distance on the experience does not aid him. Once he has traveled to his new position in Cumberland and had a full night's sleep, things are no better as his control over perceptions, memories, and time are called into question: "A confused sensation having suddenly lost my familiarity with the past, without acquiring any additional clearness of idea in reference to the present or the future, took possession of my mind" (57). The shock of meeting the woman in white at midnight and not understanding whether she is a dream or real and, if real, whether she is nervous, mad, or a victim of false imprisonment in an asylum appears to subject Walter's mind and authority to stress. He is all the more susceptible from her "touch" (47) to being touched by Laura Fairlie.

As the story continues, Walter's heart becomes devoted to Laura, but in a novel that names its heroine after a Petrarchan love object and plays on the name of its self-identified hero, one is left to wonder about our teller's head and heart and his "right" seeing. Ordinary evidence, maxims, impressions, and cultural associations proceed to be contradicted as Harwright's authority is shown to reside in excessive passivity, a growing nervousness, and an increasing inability to process the very disruptions that occur all around and within him. A fuller examination of the novel would confirm that Hartright, the presumed hero, becomes more like the outsiders Fosco and Marian as the novel unfolds—learning to see better and more. He has had to flee to Honduras, where (like Marian) he has suffered a fever and been near death, before he returns. Now practicing stratagems like stealth walking that he first learned "against suspected treachery in the wilds of Central America" (474), Hartright becomes, like them, calculating. Like a Marian who clings dangerously to a roof, drenched in the rain, spying on Fosco and Percival and like a Fosco who operates outside conventions and the law, Hartright now calls not on the police for help in London, but on an anarchist Pesca. He achieves a restoration of Laura's identity outside the law; by pure chance he is responsible for Fosco's death.[20]

Articulated as a challenge to a temporal understanding of narrative, objectivity, and the increasing presence granted in the nineteenth century to a psychologized, subjective view, *The Woman in White* moves back and forth among points of view, while ironizing, qualifying, and disqualifying "evidence." Collins reveals the delusions, fantasies, and illusion or projection-bound nature of truth and identity, while drawing on contemporary frameworks for explanation from physiognomy to the pathologization of a nervousness culturally constructed as female.

Collins's emphasis on narrative shock tactics and his deployment of multiple and distinct discursive modes—preamble, diary, letter, dream, tombstone, inscription, and manuscript—draw attention to the social constructedness of the text and the seeking for control over writing. His use of multiple narrative modes—first person, third person omniscience, and free indirect discourse—with multiple tellers translates content into a dramatic performativity. Each teller and perspective is itself, as in the poetry of Robert Browning, put on trial by a reader. Collins, I would submit, implies that fragmentary sensations and pieces of knowledge are all we have in both life and art. Perspectives are limited and partial, but so is the truth we seek. The only truth is the suspension of disbelief necessary for the success of the fiction. And success of the fiction depends upon a play (in the sense of game as well as movement) of perspectives. Moreover, truth is often dull where untruth can be intriguing; if we have mysteries such as the woman in white to thrill us, we may never have nor need the full truth.

Through Hartright first, but not last, Collins questions numerous forms of authority: patriarchal, legal, medical, textual, visual. Collins offers two portraits of women who look the same and points out that a lover-painter, the authorities, and the reader cannot tell them apart. By placing a madwoman at the heart of his text, he critiques dominant modes of looking and knowing as strongly as George Eliot would soon do by privileging her confused, cataleptic weaver, Silas Marner. By restoring Laura to her rightful place, as Browning had done with Pippa, and by having a secret brotherhood killer knife Fosco to death, Collins emphasizes chance as a far more significant determinant than the character traits of patience or resolution his narrative is supposedly meant to validate (33).

In "Pippa Passes," also the story of a young woman whose identity is stolen, Browning tries to restore a providential order. Pippa may be condemned to work in a factory; she is threatened to die an early death by Bluefox. Yet she may be reinstated to both her fortune and her identity when the Monsignor acknowledges her as his brother's daughter. Browning, then, is still comfortable in drawing on religion to reorder the accidentality of his plot. Yet Collins features no clerical figure to rescue Laura. The power of the church lies in its registries and tombstones and destruction by fire. The only clergyman in Collins's book is the one Anne Catherick's mother imagines will bow to her (560). Importing Italian ruffians into an English drama of stolen identity, Collins implies that a providential order no longer operates in the English novel. Fosco, not Hartright, best understands this new, alien reality.

Whereas George Eliot will uphold the truth of feeling in *Silas Marner*, no matter how she challenges it, Collins ironizes those who present themselves as feeling. While she will validate that truth of feeling by punishing Godfrey Cass through causal and predictable events, Collins eschews such validation. There is no truth of feeling, only of sensation, no substance, only frisson. Glyde and Fosco are punished, to be sure, but by sheer accident. On another day at another time, one might have escaped fire and the other the knife thrust. Despite its distrust of fictional ordering and its challenge to both omniscient and subjective points of view, *The Woman in White* offers the reader a tentative role of responsibility and a role of authority. Yet the novel's constant circling of deferral and referral also deprives the reader of that role again and again. Near the end of the narrative, Hartright pulls the rug out from under the reader with an admission so damaging to his authority that it also reveals our own pretensions. Hartright makes the fictional aspect of the narrative an open secret by explaining that for the sake of Laura's reputation he has been telling the story under feigned names (563). The fiction we have been reading has implicated our own credulity.

Thus, his name is not even Hartright, nor hers Fairlie. Could it be that the villain was not even Italian after all? We can now read Walter as a Collins-like ironist who plays with his own idealizations. Was his point of view truly as earnest as we had been led to assume? Were his declared motives even true? What is the status of the truth he wishes to piece together? Largely ignored by critics of the novel, his imposture may have unexpected ramifications.

In the final scene, one as provocative as Walter's vision of Laura by her own grave, Marian Halcombe playfully introduces "two eminent personages," "Mr. Walter Hartright" and "the heir of Limmeridge," Walter his son (646). By having father and son share the same feigned name, Collins raises the possibility that the novel's ending stresses Walter Hartright's enhanced financial situation as much as six-month-old Walter's succession to Frederick Fairlie's property. The status of telling is questioned to such a degree by the novel, then, that one is left to ask if Hartright is quite so innocent as his self-construction has implied. He too has perpetrated a fraud. Maybe Fosco, the man in black, can write a novel from a perspective that more credibly counters the incredible narrative of the self-righteous husband of a woman in white.

EXPANSIONS AND LIMITS OF VISION
IN *SILAS MARNER*

For novelists, omniscient narration, in which a third-person narrator moves around freely in time and place, with a bird's eye view into and out of the minds of characters, becomes the equivalent of the single mastering gaze, a literary agent in apparent godlike control of the real.[21] Yet George Eliot's third-person narrators differ and develop in each novel she writes, and it is especially important to understand how advanced she was in her thinking when she published *Silas Marner* in 1861. Some time ago, George Levine located a turn in George Eliot's faith in external reality. He targeted *Romola* (1862–63), as beginning "a process of intensified recognition of the difficulties of knowing" explored through all her later fiction (1980, 3). This recognition is already pronounced in *Silas Marner*, however, which takes up the issue of perception and interpretation as directly as Browning had done, but this time in the case of a cataleptic weaver.

George Eliot's exploration occurs on many levels of the fiction—in a remarkably sophisticated construction of her narrator, in a central character prone to loss of consciousness, in a double dialogic plot structure, in showing sympathizers as themselves limited, and in a full, diegetic exploration of different perspectives on life, especially in the scene of the Rainbow Inn. Eliminating the need to have one point of view at the expense of another, this novel accepts multiple points of view and differing capacities for taking in and interpreting what one sees, as it both expands and limits the capabilities of point of view.

If the window is the emblem for complicating perspective in "Pippa Passes," the rainbow serves that function in this novel. As George Eliot deploys it, the name "Rainbow" for the inn of Raveloe where villagers gather to relax, drink, and talk, refers to the sign of the Noahitic Covenant, made after the devastation of the flood (Genesis 9:13, 15), promising a new beginning. She employs it in a parable of the destruction of part of Silas's life in Lantern Yard and of his eventual redemption and new life through Eppie, who appears to him as a vision of golden light after an episode of catalepsy. However, Eliot's equally important reference is to a natural, physical phenomenon concerning vision, light, and perception. George Eliot was familiar with the science of natural phenomena through her reading and through her partner, George Henry Lewes. In 1635 Descartes had first analyzed the details of rainbow formation, discovering that a rainbow forms when two quite different natural phenomena, raindrops and sunshine, cross paths. When light passes through droplets, it is refracted and reflected off their insides—separating the light into its colors along concentric rays, rather like a prism. The bow is an illusion, a cone cut off by the horizon line. There is no end to a rainbow, and no vanishing point. For a rainbow is measured from the observer's eye, and it moves as the observer moves; no two people see exactly the same rainbow.

While the rainbow is an image stressing optical perception, George Eliot draws on its literal, symbolic, and metaphorical meanings. She suggests that vision and perception are like a rainbow—with no natural vanishing point. Her selection of the rainbow is also a commentary on the distortions that are central to much of how and what we see, distortions governed in large part by where we stand (literally or figuratively). Finally, she extends its meaning metaphorically to include the object we see that vanishes even as we look at it, the object that also is not fixed.

It is noteworthy that just before she embarked on *Silas Marner,* George Eliot had relied on a first-person narrator in the anonymously published *The Lifted Veil* (1859). The speaker Latimer, with an ability to see into the minds of others and to predict the future, including his own death, is blessed or cursed. His power as a narrator resembles that of a third-person narrator who can overhear characters' thoughts and forecast their futures. Whatever else Latimer may mean, in addition to a figural signaling of George Eliot's fascination with the contemporary sciences of physiology and psychology, he surely represents a concern about the horrors of full omniscience. As Kate Flint puts it, "to lift the veil" means not only "to peep at the forbidden, to access taboo knowledge," but to occupy a "masculine, even a godlike position" (95). Latimer discovers that omniscience is ruinous to sympathy, because it reveals the mendacity and selfish motives of others and it uncovers gruesome futures immune to human agency. Moreover, it does not operate when he tries to penetrate the mind of the person from whom he wants the greatest sympathy: Bertha, a murderous, hateful, unredeemable "other." Almost until the end of her career, both George Eliot and her editor John Blackwood "thought it best not to acknowledge the authorship of that strange tale about a diseased visionary cursed with the power of seeing beyond the 'veil' of reality" (Knoepflmacher 1968, 129). The monstrousness of the novella could disturb a mass readership, because it was so seemingly at odds with George Eliot's reputation as a realist.

Continuing her exploration of consciousness and vision, but attacking problems of knowing through a third-person narrator in *Silas Marner,* George Eliot sought a new "mode of presentation" (George Eliot, Haight, III: 378; Cross, II: 287). Significantly, she had originally thought of casting the story in metrical narrative poetry. Although she took her epigraph and much inspiration from William Wordsworth's "Michael," she ultimately chose the novella, parable form for her Job-like tale; and one may only speculate upon why she may not have wished to invoke comparisons with Romantic narrative poetry. My own view is that narrative poetry may have confined her into conventional expectations, thus not affording her as much scope for exploring omniscience and sympathy as she now required.

Silas as a character is the opposite of Latimer—limited, occluded in his capacity to understand others. He too, like Latimer, is subject to betrayal by one he loves. But the narrator's omniscience, though extending sympathy to Silas, now exercises her own self-limitations. An omniscient narrator's sympathy, George Eliot recognizes, must be both checked and dispersed among minor and major figures, rather than extended primarily to a single character.[22] From the marvelous opening scene which first features the active point of view of a dog and his fierce responsive barking at a bent man—"for what dog likes a figure bent under a heavy bag?" (51), a view which the narrator then shifts to his equally limited shepherd owner, George Eliot's narrator subverts both the dominance of anthropocentric impressions and expands the objective point of view. She asks her readers to recognize that animal instinct, a primitive reaction, deserves the same interpretive attention demanded by any human point of view and that it may, in fact, tell us as much as analytic reason. From the start, then, the narrator presents varieties of seeing and kinds of knowing, along a spectrum akin to a rainbow, some more limited than others, but each valuable.

Significantly, this omniscient narrator, who assumes the self-conscious "I" at critical moments, mixes a perspective that is both optical and based in the senses in a novel in which a reliable or unified field of vision is presented as an impossibility and, more importantly, as undesirable, even this early in her writing career. Influenced by George Henry Lewes's studies in *The Physiology of Common Life* (1859), George Eliot plumbs the relationships of the visible and invisible, promoting the importance of the perceptual, instinctive, and imaginative as necessary and superior to the optical alone.[23] Her Wordsworthian distrust of a pictorialism enlisting only the outer eye, a distrust shared by Ruskin and Turner, pushes her realism into aural, dramatic, corporeal, and symbolic domains.[24] Importantly, *Silas Marner* differs from George Eliot's previous fictions because of its relatively diminished pictorialism. George Henry Lewes believed that the organic interaction among the senses involved in perception undercut the Cartesian division between mind and body and the identification of the self with conscious, rational thought which that theory sustained (Shuttleworth 23). Adopting these lessons of science, art, and poetry for her fiction, George Eliot has her omniscient narrator rely on the interaction of optics, sense impressions, and imaginative insight to involve the reader in a multidimensional act of seeing.

By way of example, in the opening of chapter 2, George Eliot's narrator invokes "even people whose lives have been made various by learning" (62), who might be presumed to have reserves of adaptability, yet who, like Silas, suffer a common experience of exile when ripped from the past and thrust into new circumstances. Even "their experience," suggests the narrator, "may hardly enable them thoroughly to imagine what was the effect on a simple weaver like Silas Marner, when he left his own country people and came to settle in Raveloe" (63). In fact, she maintains, their learning may not serve, but actually may impede their ability to imagine the effect on a simple weaver. On one hand, since she is telling the story, the narrator suggests she does have this power of imagination. On the other hand, by calling attention to the limits imposed by knowledge, the narrator fully accepts the boundaries of her own experience and instincts, too, as she refuses to claim full knowledge of another's suffering.

In fact, the case of the cataleptic weaver may be one without an expert. No individual may be able to understand the effect on Silas of the catastrophes that occurred in his life in Lantern Yard and his subsequent transplantation in Raveloe. The narrator's interpellation of the reader here is not aimed at our identification with a character or with a point of view or even with a situation; it is far more demanding a novelistic request and far more generous towards the object of vision. It is an interpellation that engages us through our own blind spot.

We might trust, with Adam Smith, that only if we have imagined the position of another could we truly understand or judge a situation. But this is not a sentimental tale; it is a parable that balances realism, skepticism, and fantasy. George Eliot's narrator goes further than Smith: even if we have inhabited the position of another, we may still be unable to grasp that person's situation. The narrator insists that identification with a situation or position does not equal identity. Moreover, Eliot seems to anticipate what would become more obvious in the twentieth century: some positions are so appalling as to be unable to be imagined, no matter how sympathetic the observer. In a novel that establishes the character of Silas Marner as a dis-unified psychological subject, suffering gaps in consciousness, the narrator questions any putative single or monological authority granted to her or assumed by anyone else.

A dual allegiance marks the narrator, who represents herself as both an omniscient "narrative consensus" (Ermarth 1985, 76) or a "collective mind" (Miller 63–67), at the same time that she represents an individual. If, according to Lewes, the social is ultimately a function of varying perspectives that arrive at a temporary consensus (in sympathy for Silas, we all have a sense of exile), the singular perspective (in this case, the narrator's) remains itself in a dialogic struggle between a socially inscribed self (common experience) and an individual self (with experiences fully shaped by but not identical to common experience), neither of which is automatically adequate to each new situation.

In that struggle, communities fail to see, individuals fail to see. The community of Lantern Yard is rigid; that of Raveloe is short-sighted. Neither Silas nor Godfrey is able to "measure" even people with whom they "had lived so long" because of human "error" (224). The narrator too must navigate among multiple kinds of seeing and perceiving: psychological, physiological, sensual, imaginative. For George Eliot, a complex and unpredictable negotiation thus takes place in any embodied understanding of seeing and knowing as the dialogic struggle of her narrator is one with limit itself, with the burden of a perception that is at times not enough and at other times too great. Her challenge as an artist is not to predict the outcome of such individual negotiations, but to illustrate them for a reader, while at the same time, she frames them in terms of struggle and mystery, not solution. If she is the "professional sympathy extender" claimed by James Buzard (283), and she surely is, I would argue that as early as 1859 she is fully aware of the limits of sympathy, of the stakes of extending sympathy, and of the dangers of her profession.

In her own writings on omniscient authority and narration, George Eliot shows herself to be suspicious of the strict control or moralizing some of her critics have imputed to her narrators.[25] Presented as a pseudo-historian, the narrator of her novels always relies on a specific, rather than a universal, viewpoint. Indeed, she does not share in assumptions of a single theory of reality or epistemological certainties.[26] Moreover, George Eliot's fiction insists that knowledge is not possessed by any single class, sex, gender, sect, or nation. Neither character nor reader is ever allowed to take refuge in an insular or an untested knowledge, precisely because reality can be known, if at all, only through a dialogue of objectivity and subjectivity.

As *Silas Marner* repeatedly illustrates, a limited point of view is not to be automatically taken as deficient. For example, the moments when Silas succumbs to a cataleptic fit erase perspective and point of view altogether, creating gaps of knowledge for the character and confusion among others when reported or witnessed. These gaps, which momentarily annul routine time and space, like the moment of Annunciation set in secular context in Rossetti's painting *The Girlhood of Mary Virgin*, are moments of violence and arrival (the stealing of the gold, the arrival of a child). They are also moments of blindness, such as the blinding evoked in the Turner paintings discussed in chapter 1, which serve literally and emblematically to throw into question the validity of sight. By doing away with a normalized point of view based in a shared reality, the representation of a disabled consciousness opens up a reader's receptivity to alternate modes of vision. This limited vision is a boon—Silas's sympathy for the infant Eppie is based in the senses and not reasoned or analytical as the narrator's always has to be. Moreover, although Silas's seizures appear to stem from a verifiable medical condition, they serve as a wry commentary on psychic and social sureties in all the characters and institutions represented in the book.

Perhaps more to the point, George Eliot's novel mocks the chief character-sympathizer in Raveloe. Closest to the narrator in function, Dolly Winthrop, the wheelwright's wife, a "mild, patient woman" (133), is praised for her "conscience." Like a Smithean observer, she views the case of Silas Marner. Yet she receives the narrator's irony as well, for it was her nature, says the omniscient narrator, "to seek out all the sadder and more serious elements of life, and *pasture her mind upon them*" (134; my emphasis). Dolly's point of view is not limited only because of class or station or intellect level, then, but because along with her ability to see the vulnerability of others, she harbors exactly what makes sympathizers seek to sympathize—she seeks to help. She is a figure whom the reader and narrator like immensely. The narrator is at pains to point out that Dolly is not superior in wisdom. She is not like the narrator. She does not even know what I.H.S. means when she stamps the symbolic letters on her lard cakes. Ignorant though she may be, however, her point of view is valued greatly because she shares the narrator's sympathy. The narrator will not, however, let sympathy itself go unchecked in Dolly or herself. In ironizing Dolly as an obsessive sensibility, the narrator points out a sympathizer's strong desire to graze and feast on victims for the chance of extending fellow feeling. Sympathy is not without its distortions.

In addition, the double plots of Silas Marner and Godfrey Cass, each narrative strand a commentary on the other, reinforce the arbitrariness of a single life or a single way of looking at reality, despite the narrator's 'comprehensive' vision. The narrator opposes the limited worldview of Godfrey Cass to that of the equally nearsighted Silas Marner, while emphasizing the strengths of each. The novel exquisitely turns on the chance connections between Silas Marner and Godfrey Cass, very different men, each flawed, passive, and suffering. These connections are made first through Dunstan Cass, Godfrey's brother, who steals Silas's gold, and later through Eppie, Godfrey's illegitimate child; they are connected through the omniscient point of view.[27]

Yet, despite two plots and two very different perspectives on reality, what is often taken as an opposition of fates is immediately complicated by the narrator's inclusions—which defeat a single perspective on either. The reader is refused the ease of focusing on one to the detriment of the other and is blocked in assigning simple explanations to each case. If we associate Marner's fate with accident and chance, we have to take account of the chance death of Molly in the snow, an event which suddenly frees Godfrey to marry Nancy Lammeter. We also must note that the chance finding of Dunstan in the stone pits finally seems to impel Godfrey to own up to his fatherhood of Eppie. If we associate free will with Godfrey's turning aside from his responsibilities earlier towards Molly Farren, towards Eppie, and towards Nancy, do we not also have to associate free will with the dogged persistence with which Silas chooses to bury his past? His repression of earlier memories allows him to become so wedded to his loom that he loses human characteristics and becomes rigidly part of the machine. If we associate ignorance with Marner, who cannot fathom the evil of his friend William Dane, do we not also have to associate ignorance with Godfrey, who cannot fathom the evil of his brother or the goodness of his wife Nancy? Discovering that Nancy would have adopted Eppie as her own daughter, sixteen years earlier, for instance, "Godfrey felt the bitterness of an error . . . he had not measured his wife with whom he had lived so long" (224). George Eliot sets up the opposition only to deconstruct it into a persistently tested and qualified dialogue. By offering two men, equally flawed, equally prone to error and to chance, and equally converted to better ways, George Eliot uses a conscious structuring of character and plot to demolish fixed perspective.

Throughout *Silas Marner*, the omniscient narrator features different explanations of reality and different perspectives for her reader to weigh and sort in addition to those driving her double plot. Perspectives are questioned even as they are uttered by a careful juxtaposition to other, different views. Lantern Yard's belief in a Puritan God of retribution is one point of view. Silas's excommunication and subsequent loss of faith, which result in his search for a meaning in the ritualistic patterns of daily life, is another point of view. Yet in this comparison, neither perspective is much better than the other, since both are rigidly applied.

Other comparisons yield hierarchy, privileging perspectives even when (or most assuredly when) they are patchworked and provisional rather than whole or certain. Counterpointed to her husband's blind trust in chance, Nancy Lammeter's belief in a theology by which she conducts her life, "pieced together" as it is out of social traditions, "girlish reasonings" (217), and doctrine "imperfectly understood," is fragmentary. Yet the very piecemeal nature of this "knowledge," akin to a natural growing organism, is more valuable than his because it eludes systematization. Nancy's imperfect faith amounts to what George Eliot's narrator terms a "moral sensibility" (214). Dolly Winthrop, in turn, believes intuitively in a cosmic order in which cycles occur regularly, many things are "dark to us"; yet she avers that we should trust in a larger plan (179, 241). Only through such shifting and testing of varied institutional, codified, and individual points of view offered by the narrator, within the narrative voice and between the characters, do we arrive at a post-perspectival knowledge.

To be sure, the omniscient third-person narrator states firm observations, when, for instance, declaring that Godfrey's "imagination constantly created an alibi for Dunstan" (128). Or, again when pondering why the temporal coincidence of Dunstan's disappearance and Silas's robbery went entirely unnoticed in Raveloe, she maintains: "I doubt whether a combination so injurious to the prescriptive respectability of a family with a mural monument and venerable tankards, would not have been suppressed as of unsound tendency" (128). Nevertheless, despite such occasional judicial interventions, an authoritative voice of maxims or wisdom is rare here, as it would be inimical to the novel's emphasis on the necessity of a multiplicity of perspectives.

Nor is there resolution at the end of the novel offering a full view of what happened to each man. While the corpse of Dunstan is exhumed, other buried pasts remain buried. Pictorially, morally, and in terms of omniscient narration, the line between the present and the distant past has been irretrievably broken. Silas may have achieved "a consciousness of unity between his past and present" (202) through Eppie, but he can never right the wrongs perpetrated against him in Lantern Yard. He can neither seek nor gain justice. We do not know if the truth ever emerged. The district itself is erased (see Davis 153). Raveloe, a sixteenth-century English word which means both "to untangle, unwind" and "to become tangled or confused," defies a reader's search for elucidation.[28]

In the well-known sixth chapter of *Silas Marner*, in the aptly named Rainbow Inn, a scene always praised for its local dialect and humor, George Eliot most powerfully explores multiple interpretations. Oppositional attitudes about causality in each of the topics of discussion are resolved by Mr. Snell, the landlord "of neutral position" (95) who opines that positions are both right and wrong and that truth lies between. The topics covered include the material, the immaterial, the legal bond, and the invisible. The exchange suggests that no absolute standards of judgment exist and that neither clinging to the material nor belief in the immaterial offers a promise of reliability.[29]

If the rainbow indicates the refraction of points of view in the scene and in the world of the novel as a whole, *Silas Marner* solves the problem of objective realism by leaving it unresolved. The novel's solution, instead, is handled dramatically in Eppie's choice to stay with Silas, rather than join her real father, Godfrey. This solution is based on the same two elements the novel so dramatically opposed through the double plot: chance and free will.[30] The chance that a subjective point of view can be exercised with free will and be a good decision, given certain circumstances, remains the point of the novel. There is no single satisfactory objective point of view, which is why the last word is given not to the narrator but to Eppie and pivots on reciprocal regard: "I think nobody could be happier than we are" (244).

Silas Marner thus challenges a single, omniscient point of view on various grounds, revising the sentimental case while doing so. It offers multiple layers of refracted and reflected points of view about the Divine, causality, and interpretation. It makes the light-fracturing rainbow and the shock of a new perspective after a state of blank seizure governing metaphors for perception. Ultimately, though, the novel cares less about what we see or know and more about how we choose to act on the partial subjective view we take, with the information we happen to have. Eliot does not rely on omniscient narrative authority or on an unchecked sympathy. If she did there would be no singularity, no differentiation, and no ability to discriminate among points of view. Indeed, limiting sympathy is the only way sympathy can be maintained.

The narrator of *Middlemarch,* the syncretic masterpiece that George Eliot published in 1871–72, derides our tendency to read—and interpret—cultural productions as isolated in "box-like partitions without vital connection" (157). Indeed, this same narrator had opened her rich "Study of Provincial Life" by immediately yoking visual and literary coordinates. She shapes our initial perception of Dorothea Brooke's dignified appearance by alluding both to the "Italian painters" who depicted "The Blessed Virgin" as well as to "a fine quotation from the Bible—or from one of our elder poets,—in a paragraph of today's newspapers" (5). George Eliot's readers thus are promptly schooled: only by responding to multiple perspectives, can they adopt the desirable elasticity of a "mind flexible with constant comparison" (157).

Written for a series of short books intending to provoke debate, *Perspectives* contends that only the flexibility of a cross-generic approach can allow us to appreciate the full importance of the formal innovations that took place in Victorian England from the 1830s to the 1870s. The case studies I present—of paintings and poems, of photographs and novels, as well as nonfictional essays—offer side-by-side visual and textual readings that should substantiate my contention that perspective became a dominant issue in early-nineteenth-century cultural sites, across different genres and media. My analyses of works by Turner, Dyce, Tennyson, Browning, Morris, D. G. Rossetti, Robinson, Hawarden, Collins, and George Eliot thus should be read as partial soundings within a much larger narrative of connections among the literary and visual arts. The layerings of perception in Romantic poetry and the earliest uses of free indirect discourse in the novel at the end of the eighteenth century had innovatively linked consciousness to form. But the Victorians, who lived in a type-filled, text-filled era, in which print and art reproductions multiplied at an increasing pace, were responsible for converting perspective into a prime metaphor not only for epistemology but for a highly self-conscious hermeneutics.

In handling the large topic of perspective, I have made specific delimiting choices. Instead of selecting objects for study that were unusual or unknown, I have purposely chosen well-known texts with the aim of teasing out complications of perspective and point of view. I have also purposely resisted current notions linking formalism to cultural studies that label literary or aesthetic form as the same as or inferior to other cultural forms (Rooney 35; Levine 2006, 635). Although I intervene in scholarly debates about epistemology, art history, form and cultural politics, optics, and the importance of technology, I have resisted weighting down a slim book with theoretical freight. Instead of extending my analyses to empire and colony, I have resolutely concentrated on the metropole. My emphasis has been preeminently dialogical. I am interested in dialogue within a text, across and between paired texts, and between the text or art object and an interpellated reader-viewer. Here the dramatic monologue of the 1830s, a form original to the Victorians, which threw into new relief the drama of subjectivity by stressing contradiction, revision, and incompleteness, provided me with the perfect mental springboard for my readings of other forms.

A much longer and more historically grounded book has yet to be written that will combat the still prevalent rupture theory of Modernism by building on the case studies I discuss. But I am less interested here in constructing the Victorians as protomodernists or postmodernists than in promoting the interdisciplinary and intergeneric approach that allowed me to locate a fundamental element common to the works I discuss, while maintaining the distinctive linguistic and imagistic qualities among very different kinds of aesthetic, cultural constructions. The self-consciousness, hybridity, and multiplicity of Victorian forms that so persistently enact a variety of perspective paradigms call upon varieties of interpretive strategies from their viewer-readers. In treating poetry, fictional and nonfictional prose, photography, and painting, I here write against the firm divisions maintained so often by historicist and formalist critics and insist that the shape of the nineteenth-century cultural field and the contours of developing media and genres must be appreciated across divisions. At the same time, I have attempted not to deny or collapse the crucial, salient differences among individual art works.

INTRODUCTION

1. I will interchangeably use the terms Renaissance, classical, and linear perspective.

2. Art historians may complicate such a judgment, and artists themselves may never have subscribed wholly to geometric perspective in any historical period.

3. Elkins has classified common "others" to linear perspective, including anamorphosis, reverse perspective, inverted perspective, curvilinear perspective, herringbone perspective, stereoscopic perspective, anaglyphs, hyperbolic perspective, engineering drawing, and others. Leonardo da Vinci is known for atmospheric perspective or *sfumato*—a technique of layering in order to create a blurring effect without lines or borders. Significantly, these "others" do not overturn linear perspective, even if troubling it (see Elkins 1994, 117, 146–53).

4. Panofsky believed perspective offered access to a world that could be known. Poststructuralist theory, whether formulated by Lacan, Foucault, Saussure, Harraway, or others, shows itself to be fascinated by and concerned by ocularcentric culture, but—as is well known—discredits an all-seeing eye as an avenue to knowing in favor of partial perspectives or situated knowledges. Theorists Damisch and Grootenboer explain perspective as a signifying system, a network that gives meaning, not a sign that means (Grootenboer 122).

5. Massey maintains that the association is never based on a close reading of Descartes. Work of the 1990s illustrated that the cogito is not conceived only in terms of a dualistic, spatial configuration or as a single, static perspective.

6. Merleau-Ponty locates a break with the disembodied viewing associated with traditional perspective with Cézanne (Merleau-Ponty, "Cézanne's Doubt" (1992), 15; and see Jay 1993, 159). While also citing modernism as a break, James Krasner importantly notes that "it is clear that the interiority of modernist narrative can be traced to an empirical tradition shared by Darwin" (5).

7. The comments of Auerbach have been highly influential. "The Brown Stocking" opens with a lengthy quotation from *To the Lighthouse* (1929) to establish that "the writer as narrator of objective facts has almost completely vanished; almost

everything stated appears by way of reflection in the consciousness of the dramatic personae" (471–72).

8. As may be clear from other sources referenced, Foucault, Debord, and Benjamin remain central to the study of perspective and modernities. For classic readings in visual culture, see Mirzoeff 1998.

9. See Mitchell 1986. The relationship of picture to word has a long history of criticism. For two modern, well-known examples from within the discipline of art history, see Alpers and Fried.

10. While critique can allow for new ideas that might shift cultural understandings and self-awareness, and make room in Raymond Williams's terms for 'emergent' forms, it does not guarantee subversion of dominant norms or social change. The distinction is made, without the connection to Williams, by Slinn in 2003b, 29. A cultural critique can only be partial, for it still supports, to some degree, the very norms it exposes by virtue of the fact that it remains embedded in ideology.

11. See Didi-Huberman; Bal 1996; Elkins 1996; and Mitchell 1986, 37–40. A recent research project in the Netherlands, "The Pensive Image," studied further the extent to which images (painting, photography, cinema, etc.) are able to philosophize on the nature of vision and on the status of their own representation. It is based on the hypothesis that "monocular models of vision such as perspective and the camera have shaped our binocular perception of the world." Downloaded May 18, 2006 from http://www.janvaneyck.nl/0_2_3_events_info/arc_06_the pensiveimage_symposium.html

12. See Shires.

CHAPTER 1

1. The relationship of literature to the visual arts in the nineteenth century has been extensively documented. See Praz; Tinker; Meyers; Mitchell 1977; Altick; Miller 1992; Green-Lewis; Byerly; Wolfson; Schwartz and Przyblyski; Andres; Psomiades 1997. On representation, see Mitchell 1994 and Marin.

2. Carol T. Christ and John O. Jordan conclude that "the Victorians were interested in the conflict, even the competition, between objective and subjective paradigms for perception," xxiii.

3. Green-Lewis 26–27.

4. Bal 1996, 182.

5. Bhabha 111. Thus with regard to visual culture, spectators are also the spectacle. With regard to verbal culture, readers are also the text. Shelly Vye, writing on nineteenth-century tourism, puts it this way: hybridity is "the complex intersections of cultures and subjectivities, lived neither as mimesis nor pure difference" (6). In Lacanian terms with regard to visuality, the gaze is produced from a position exterior to the subject. The look of the other outside the self, whether real or imagined, is integral to the exercise of the spectatorial gaze and yet also constitutive of a spectator's picture of him or herself. To be seen as a viewing subject means to imagine how one would be seen viewing from the position of an other, a position that one will never occupy. Slavoj Žižek elucidates in terms of pictures: "The gaze marks the point in the object (in the picture) from which the subject

viewing it is already gazed at, i.e., it is the object that is gazing at me. . . . The gaze is, so to speak, a point at which the very frame of my view is already inscribed in the 'content' of the picture viewed," as quoted by Vye 498–49, from *Looking Awry* 126.

6. See L. Smith; I. Armstrong 1993.

7. John Ruskin, as note 1, *Turner*, vol. 13, 136.

8. Miller 1992, 112. Paulson sees a conflict between graphic and verbal in Turner's work (167–88). Taking issue, J. Hillis Miller maintains that Turner does not always feature graphic over verbal, nor does his art always make the graphic subversive (1992, 112).

9. John Gage, *Colour in Turner* (1969) as quoted in *Turner 1975–1851*, 133.

10. I'm grateful to Mike Goode for his question about irony and Turner's artistic authority.

11. As quoted in *Turner, 1775–1851*, 134. On critical reception of Turner's paintings and poems, see Lindsay, 124–26, 169–72 and Wilton 68.

12. Johann Wolfgang von Goethe published *Zur Farbenlehre*, translated by Sir Charles Eastlake as *Goethe's Theory of Colours* in 1840. Goethe had studied afterimages, retinal aftereffects from staring at the sun, and concluded that they proved the eye was not merely a passive receiver. For the eye seemed to have its own internal lights and color effects as well as those which it perceived. Moreover, he believed that colors were intrinsic aspects of material objects and not just reflected on them. This work critically influenced Eastlake's friend Turner though members of the Royal Academy were split over the importance of color theories (see Kemp, as note 3, 298–99). Kemp notes the very different theories of seeing and reality put forward later by the influential optical scientist Hermann von Helmholtz in *Handbuch der physiologischen Optik* (1856–66), who was held in esteem during the second half of the nineteenth century. Helmholtz emphasizes the interpretive act of seeing over a pattern of physical stimuli, whereas Ruskin's theory centers on a tension between visual and cerebral factors (243). See Tim Barringer 59. Crary uses Turner's "Colour—Goethe's Theory . . . " to support his argument for the emergence of the embodied modern observer (1992, 141). J. Hillis Miller views the paintings as a "punning self-portrait and hyperbolic Promethean or Apollonian boast of the painter's heliotropic power as turner [*sic*]" (1992, 144). Notably, when Turner was asked to explain the paintings, he is reputed to have replied to Ruskin: "red, blue and yellow"—referring to the traditional primary colors.

13. On this point, see Charles Taylor 368 and Wahrman 294, both of whom point to the broader cultural forces surrounding Romanticism—so as precisely to avoid claiming the priority of one cultural domain over another. As Wahrman puts it, a "pervasive set of intersecting concerns, theories, readings, and key terms extended far beyond the horizons of scientists and literary writers alike."

14. Tucker (1984, 121–37) draws out the play of self against context here and gives a wonderfully nuanced reading not only of Tennyson's first dramatic monologue but also of Browning's "Madhouse Cells," pendants in which "a lyric drive collects itself only to furnish the impetus for its own overthrow. In such martial arts of discrediting the lyric 'I,' Browning had no peer" (126), though, as Tucker shows, he had a predecessor in the Tennyson of "St. Simeon Stylites."

15. I. Armstrong 1982, xiii. Armstrong has argued convincingly (1993, especially 13–19) for the Victorian poem as a *double poem* in which lyric expressivity and

dramatized observation of, reflection on, or commentary on that expressivity are in a tension and constant redefinition.

16. Among Charles Dickens's *Sketches by Boz* (1836), we find the story (Tales, IV) of a Mr. Tuggs, a London grocer who, on a trip to Ramsgate with his family, takes an excursion to Pegwell Bay. They travel around by donkey, lunch at the hotel there known for its delicious shrimp, and explore at the bottom of the cliffs, looking at crabs, seaweed, and eels.

17. For brief discussion of the painting and a reproduction see: http://www.tate.org.uk/servlet/ViewWork?workid=4063, downloaded May 22, 2006.

18. Armstrong 1993, 7. See also Johnson and Langbaum.

19. On mask lyric, see Rader 140, 141.

20. Hallam in Houghton and Stange 859.

21. L. Smith 85.

22. A recent projection of colors onto the figures, visible during *son et lumière* summer showings, creates the sense of moving, living, breathing groups of saints emerging from deep recesses. This projection allows the exterior stone carvings to turn into live bodies in procession, as the interior wood carvings no doubt already did for Morris's inner eye.

23. On the physicality of textual marks, see Johanna Drucker and Jerome McGann; and see Helsinger.

CHAPTER 2

1. D. G. Rossetti, as quoted in Sharp 1882, 406.

2. Surtees 11. The first sonnet was published in *Catalogue of the Association for Promoting the Free Exhibition of Modern Art* (Gallery, Hyde Park Corner, 1849) 18 as part of catalog entry 368. The second sonnet, according to William Michael Rossetti, was printed on gilded paper with the first sonnet and it was attached to the frame; see the Rossetti Archive. Like Holman Hunt and John Millais, Rossetti intended to first show his painting at the spring exhibition in April at the Royal Academy, but changed his mind (perhaps, Faxon suggests, because he feared rejection by the Academy selection committee, 52). In 1864 the painting was reframed, at which time Rossetti had the two sonnets inscribed next to each other on the frame below the painting, which is how it would have been seen at the Royal Academy in 1883 and in subsequent hangings. The gold-covered paper did not turn up in the Tate Gallery when the picture arrived there. Rossetti's sonnets on gold paper seem not to have been an isolated instance, however. James McNeill Whistler had Algernon Swinburne's "Before the Mirror" printed on gold paper and pasted onto the frame of the painting that inspired it: the 1864 *The Little White Girl*, later also known as *Symphony in White, No. 2*. The second part of the title was added to reinforce the importance of reading the painting against mimesis as an arrangement of colors evoking a mood. (Also see chapter 3 on this set of texts in connection with Lady Hawarden's photographs.)

3. It is important to establish this as a mobile and attentive position for the viewer/reader, who is invited by this structure of sonnet and painting to read, look, reflect, gaze, and move back and forth. Most critics engaged in a discussion of mobility and spectatorship discuss visual mobility quite narrowly in terms of a

view from modern transportation vehicles or precinematic, mechanized, moving picture displays, or a glance across a surface. In "The Work of Art in the Age of Mechanical Reproduction," Benjamin contrasts the stillness with which we view a work of art with the speed of the object in film: "The painting invites the spectator to contemplation; before it the spectator can abandon himself to his associations. Before the movie he cannot do so. No sooner has his eye grasped a scene than it is already changed. It cannot be arrested" (Benjamin 240). While Benjamin's observation may still logically hold, Rossetti's double art and his invited viewer/reader complicate it. Nead smartly reassesses Benjamin's assertions in a cross-media, interdisciplinary study. Despite the fact that her research focuses on the late part of the century, two points are especially germane to this discussion: the first is that cartoons from Thomas Rowlandson in 1811 to a prominent one in *Punch* in 1906 ironize the speed with which some museum goers view art exhibitions, thus compromising the association of art with slow observation and stillness. In this context, Rossetti forces the viewer not only to move, not only to use a mobile gaze, but also to slow down. Nead further argues that movement in the modern world was characterized not by uniform speed, but by "changes in speed and direction and by acceleration, arrest, and reversal" (748). We would be hard pressed to reconstruct a nineteenth-century beholder's experience—though see Psomiades' valuable chapter 3.

4. William Fredeman argues that the sonnet form resolves problems of paintings (quoted in Stein 199). The contradictions in the sonnets, explains Stein, "become visual arrangements of separate figures or masses, to be balanced as much as in a painting" (199). While not disagreeing with Fredeman, Stein alternatively locates integration in the consciousness of the viewer/reader, where multiple perspectives are brought together. In my view, gaps and dialogic relations in consciousness, not integration, are far more congruent with Rossetti's work and with the Gothic grotesque.

5. Finch and Bowen describe Milton's pair as "unavoidably locked in a condition of textual self-consciousness where, no matter how hard each tries to extricate itself from the embrace of the other, neither can stop thinking and dreaming about its companion" (5).

6. Isobel Armstrong (2006) describes the poem as a "thesaurus of optical images." Noting that the poem draws on many lens- and mirror-based visual technologies, both old and new, Armstrong indicates that the same figure can "signify more than one optical situation." She observes that the stereoscope, about which I will have more to say in the next chapter, intervened between the 1832 and 1842 versions of the poem. Developed by David Wheatstone in 1838, it splits and reorganizes vision to produce depth and solidity in a combined (left and right) image, unlike the flat photograph. In further experimenting with perspective in 1842, Tennyson notably also dropped from his manuscript his monster-of-the-deep poem "The Kraken," which, although exploring views above and below the deep, perhaps remained too cut off from the plays of interpretation that Tennyson was beginning to encourage more fully. On mirrors and other nineteenth-century poems, see I. Armstrong 2008, 111–14.

7. On 21 November 1848, Rossetti titled the first version of the first sonnet "Mary's Girlhood (For a Picture)." He later revised the sonnet for publication in the "Sonnets for Pictures" section of the 1870 *Poems*. The sonnets exist in revised

versions on the current Tate Gallery picture frame. A full history of production and revision can be found online in the Rossetti Archive: http://www.rossettiarchive. org/docs/s40.rap.html. Downloaded October 21, 2008.

8. Through a variety of methods, including pigment samples, X-ray, and ultraviolet fluorescence microscopy, the Tate Gallery staff has established that Rossetti bought a canvas with commercially prepared, predominantly chalk, white priming, over which he layered dense lead white with some extender. He also achieved subtle textures by combining liquid, almost watercolorlike washes with flecks of stiff white paint. Having taken account of fading, wrinkling, and stiffening, the staff imagines the purple and red to have been brighter originally. It is also important to understand how much the Pre-Raphaelites depended on Goethe's color theory, mentioned earlier in connection with Turner's contrary view. See Ridge et al. 80–81 and Appendix np under "The Girlhood . . ." and "Pigments"; Kemp; and Glanville 29–38.

9. During the 1830s and 1840s, facsimiles of medieval miniatures reproduced in color and pastiche illuminated books, about which Rossetti knew through friendships with collector William Burges and John Ruskin, became plentiful. Ruskin later would also speak about the revival of religious art and its importance in his 1853 lecture "Pre-Raphaelitism." The interest in early sacred art also emerged from Anglo-Catholic Tractarians, such as Rossetti's mother and sisters. In addition, the Brotherhood members were "presumably familiar with Anna Jameson's *Sacred and Religious Art* of 1848 and Lord Lindsay's *Sketches of the History of Christian Art* of 1847, reviewed by John Ruskin in the *Quarterly Review* in June that year" (see Treuherz 155–58). In aiming to evoke a medieval context, Rossetti reminds the nineteenth-century viewer about a relationship among the image as a devotional object, the book or manuscript leaf as a devotional object, and reading practices considered as devotional practices (A. Smith 11).

10. William Bell Scott, who saw the painting in Rossetti's studio, comments: "He was painting in oils with water colour brushes, as thinly as in water-colour, on canvas which he had primed with white till the surface was as smooth as cardboard, and every tint remained transparent." See Marsh 16. The compositional scheme of an enclosed interior contrasted to an exterior glimpsed through a door, window, or other separation, and figures seemingly flattened against a wall, was common among Millais, Hunt, Hughes, and others. It was done in part to abandon chiaroscuro, and it effectively cuts off movement of the viewer's eye into space. See Landow, http://www.victorianweb.org/painting/whh/replete/finding1.html.

11. Hunt, in Marsh 315. And see Barringer. It is also important to keep in mind that "[f]ew have realized that Holman Hunt and his associates read, not the first volume of *Modern Painters*, which emphasized truth to nature, but the second volume, which contained Ruskin's theories of beauty and imagination" (Landow 1977, 317).

12. See I. Armstrong 1993, chapter 1; also see Hartman 481.

13. Though my focus is different, I am in sympathy with Griselda Pollock's 1980s wide-ranging and influential discussion of Rossetti's images of women: "Woman as sign: psychoanalytic readings" and "Woman as sign in Pre-Raphaelite literature." Pollock's narrative about vision and representation is important for placing in question kinds of cultural stereotyping. Yet I think we also need to remember Rossetti's concept of the inner standing point, put forth eloquently by

McGann in the Rossetti Archive. See note 19. Rossetti was not aiming at the power of distance between a subject and an object. See http://www.rossettiarchive.org. racs/bio-exhibit/6html (downloaded January 23, 2007).

14. Steinberg responds here to an interpretation of the painting by Snyder and Cohen. They had argued, in response to John Searle, that Velázquez's painting encourages first a misreading of perspective and then a correct secondary realization on the part of the viewer. Maintaining that multiple centers of attention are possibly intended in any painting, Steinberg suggests we resist the temptation to hierachize and narrativize them. He argues: "[T]his is not how a picture works. If two readings are allowed, then both are effectively present and ambiguously meant" (46 fn. 4).

15. This section has been informed by Anna McCarthy's work on ambient television. My thanks to Steven Cohan for bringing her argument to my attention.

16. In Rossetti's sonnet "Lost on Both Sides" from 1854, later incorporated into "The House of Life," XIC (XLIII 1870), he views each art form, the visual and the verbal, as a suitor of a woman. Suggesting that his brother composed the poem at a moment of discontent with his artistic endeavors as painter *or* poet, because he could not attain the union of the two modes he needed and desired, William Michael Rossetti helps us to understand the tremendous force of dual artistic claims on Rossetti. See Ainsworth, Introduction.

17. The Ditchley portrait of Elizabeth the First (1592) and productions of Titian and Giorgione, for instance, featured sonnets written onto the corners of both portrait and narrative paintings. Closer to Rossetti's own time, J. M. W. Turner first printed lines from his poetry manuscript "Fallacies of Hope" in the exhibit catalog to accompany the viewing of his 1812 painting *Snowstorm: Hannibal and his Army Crossing the Alps*. Rossetti thus works in a tradition long familiar to painters.

18. Mitchell importantly notes that image and text dialectics occur not just between the arts, but within them. Writing in its graphic form is a suturing of visual and verbal; as we saw in the example of Turner, the image sometimes depicts a scene from a verbal narrative, contains words on its surface, represents a kind of text, or otherwise alludes to textuality. The example of Blake is germane to Rossetti, whom he influenced. "Neither the graphic nor the poetic aspect of Blake's composite art," writes Mitchell, "assumes consistent predominance: their relationship is more like an energetic rivalry: a dialogue or dialectic between vigorously independent modes of expression." Mitchell describes the experience of conflicting aesthetic appeals in Blake's illuminated books: two equally compelling art forms, two languages, "each clamoring for primary attention" (1977, 4).

19. McGann has two especially important comments in the Rossetti Archive regarding Rossetti's interest in multiple perspective. The first is his elevation to importance of a sketch, "Venus surrounded by mirrors reflecting her in different view," for Rossetti's artistic program. A note on the sketch indicates that Rossetti had read the article on looking glasses from his copy of Smith's 1842 *Dictionary of Greek and Roman Antiquities*. McGann indicates that Rossetti's sketch is a key to the pattern of his career: a series of nonidentical views of sacred and profane love. McGann's second point about perspective is to highlight Rossetti's comments about his poem "Jenny." The infamous review-essay by Robert Buchanan (1841–1901), written under a pseudonym, Thomas Maitland, was published in the *Contemporary Review*, October 1871. Buchanan expanded the essay and published

it as a pamphlet in 1872 under the title *The Fleshly School of Poetry and Other Phenomena of the Day*. Rossetti responded to this attack with a rebuttal, "The Stealthy School of Criticism," published in the *Athenaeum* of December 1871. It is here, in talking about the poem "Jenny," that Rossetti states that he rejected a "treatment from without," or a third-person narrative about the young man and Jenny, in favor of the dramatic monologue, which features in his handling what he refers to as an "inner standing point."

> Nor did I omit to consider how far a treatment from without might here be possible. But the motive powers of art reverse the requirement of science, and demand first of all an *inner* standing-point. The heart of such a mystery as this must be plucked from the very world in which it beats or bleeds; and the beauty and pity, the self-questionings and all-questionings which it brings with it, can come with full force only from the mouth of one alive to its whole appeal, such as the speaker put forward in the poem,—that is, of a young and thoughtful man of the world. To such a speaker, many half-cynical revulsions of feeling and reverie, and a recurrent presence of the impressions of beauty (however artificial) which first brought him within such a circle of influence, would be inevitable features of the dramatic relation portrayed.

Dramatization rather than narration allows the reader to hear the speaker reveal himself in spite of himself. Thus Rossetti elicits a shifting, complex set of sympathies, emotions, and criticism from the reader, actively involving her moral imagination on not only the topic of prostitution but also on class differences, gender politics, female purity, and the economics of sexual exchange. McGann states that Rossetti first mentioned the "inner standing point" years before in an unpublished note to his pastiche poem "Ave," an early "Songs of the Art Catholic" (see McGann, Archive, Introduction).

20. See Cramer for the connection between Browning and the Pre-Raphaelites.

21. As Sharp reports in his study of Robert Browning, Rossetti had a distinctive connection to this anonymously published poem.

> One day a young poet-painter came upon a copy of the book in the British Museum Library, and was at once captivated by its beauty. One of the earliest admirers of Browning's poetry, Dante Gabriel Rossetti—for it was he—felt certain that "Pauline" could be by none other than the author of "Paracelsus." He himself informed me that he had never heard this authorship suggested, though some one had spoken to him of a poem of remarkable promise, called "Pauline," which he ought to read. If I remember aright, Rossetti told me that it was on the forenoon of the day when the "Burden of Nineveh" was begun, conceived rather, that he read this story of a soul by the soul's ablest historian. So delighted was he with it, and so strong his opinion it was by Browning, that he wrote to the poet, then in Florence, for confirmation, stating at the same time that his admiration for "Pauline" had led him to transcribe the whole of it.

Browning confirmed that Rossetti had written to him and that he had responded. http://www.worldwideschool.org/library/books/hst/biography/LifeofBrowning/chap3.html. Downloaded August 14, 2006.

22. See Robert Browning's "Essay on Percy Bysshe Shelley" (1852), in *Shelley*.

23. Pollock's point about Astarte's forward-facing engagement with the viewer is significant in reading this example of double art as cultural critique. She argues: "The dominant ideological structures within which the fetishistic regime of representation is founded are exposed and the viewer is positioned against the patriarchy" (152).

24. That Rossetti would have been attuned to such issues is clear from a note to his publisher Ellis on 27 April 1870, where he complains about the letters on the binding of the first edition of *Poems*.

Do you think that the British Fool, with the heaven-sent help of this stupendous diagram, aided by a few Michael-Angelesque throes of Composition (in the style of Solomon Hart's great picture) will be able to conceive an O and something other than a balloon, and of a T as not necessarily a gallows? Do you think he can be brought to observe the precise fitting of the letters—for instance the mighty intellect by which the P is made to fill the space pretty well? And the letters curved a little into each other and the precise thickness of the letters? In short, will he copy this, or has he a soul above it?

Doughty and Wahl, II: 856.

25. For recent commentary on Rossetti's female figures and desire: see Slinn 2003a.

CHAPTER 3

1. A narrative of historical rupture is still heard, despite efforts to complicate or silence it by Crary 1992; Jay 1993, 1996; Nead; Krauss; Gunning; and others. Victorian studies scholar Martin Hewitt argued recently in a prize-winning essay that Victorian culture writ large remained dominated by a search for truth, nurtured a hegemony of positivism, and insisted on an imperative of observation and fact collection. His narrative leads him to repeat the general assessment about photography that it "intensified pressures toward realism" (413). It is true that new technologies were often explained in terms of improving the ability to record reality (see Jay 1993, 127). This is surely but half the story—it is the story of how the Victorian upper and middle classes explained themselves and their accomplishments to themselves. How Victorians have been themselves represented is also important, and usually this reception is bifurcated. As one critic explains, the Victorians have been most commonly characterized "as positivist, imperialistic proponents of bourgeois individualism, naively (or determinedly) maintaining a belief in purely objective knowledge and absolute truth" or through their wide explorations of epistemology and interpretation, as "flawed precursors of poststructuralists" (Anger 14–15). This narrative about the nineteenth century dovetails with a much larger flawed metanarrative based in realism and temporality that dominates Western thinking and theories of narrative (see Skordili introduction). Moreover, Jonathan Loesberg was correct on October 10, 2003 on Victorialist listserv, when he noted that even while we disavow reductive histories of art and

fictional realism and aim to make our histories more complicated, "we still retain certain aspects, assumptions and traces of those histories" (membership on Indiana listserv required; archives open).

2. William Henry Fox Talbot began trying "the art of fixing a shadow" in 1833–34 (Roberts 8). Though Louis Daguerre in France had invented processes of developing photographic plates and of fixing an image in salt, the calotype invented by Talbot meant that many prints could be made from a single negative. In 1844, he published the first photographically illustrated book, *The Pencil of Nature*. Despite its original connection with alchemy and the supernatural, photography was valued in time for its truth-function, both in teaching how to see and how to regard objects (Green-Lewis 25; Roberts 9, 54). Scholars have demonstrated how in science, law enforcement, medicine, the family, and many other disciplining areas, photography came to have instrumental uses (Sekula 1986, 4–70; 1987, 121; Tagg; Foucault). Victorian verbal culture, in turn, from fiction to advertising, not only received photography in terms of realism but perpetuated discourses of verisimilitude in terms of photography (see Burgin 10 and Jay 1993, 126–27).

3. Interest in a mechanical objectivity and documentation in medicine and science increased during the period, according to Daston and Galison, as a response to *various* (my emphasis) forms of subjectivity becoming seen "as *dangerously* subjective" (82). Yet nineteenth-century visual culture was as dependent on enthusiasms such as Talbot's, as it was responsive to developing Victorian scientific discoveries. "The phenomenon which I have now briefly mentioned appears to me to partake of the character of the marvelous," Talbot wrote in the mid-1840s, "almost as much as any fact which physical investigation has yet brought to our knowledge" (2). Kate Flint and others have argued persuasively for a visual culture in the nineteenth century concerned with the unseen as much as the seen, which "unsettled expectations concerning sight and representation" (30).

4. Art photography was pictorialist in the sense that it invoked painting and dramatic tableaux to legitimize the medium of photography in an aesthetic hierarchy. It is clear that art photography was influenced by Pre-Raphaelitism, especially for fidelity to detail, as documented in Robinson's treatises. In other ways the two movements were not in tune, for example in some art photography's reliance on chiaroscuro. Art photography was begun in the 1850s. Following the introduction of the dry-plate process, pictorialism became more popular in the 1880s and declined in the early years of the twentieth century. Among methods used in nineteenth-century art photography were soft focus (Julia Margaret Cameron being the chief exponent), filters and lens coatings, manipulation in the darkroom, and various printing processes. There was a link between art photography and the developing schools of Impressionism and modern art. One of the documented connections was that, through a mutual friend, Whistler saw the photographs of Hawarden (see Lawson all; Dodier 1999, 98).

5. Importantly, Robinson is a professional whose work was widely exhibited and promoted in shop windows. Hawarden was an amateur who exhibited a small selection twice in London. Yet both were highly regarded and earned medals from the Royal Photographic Society.

6. By mid-century, scientific study of the eye and light, as well as new technologies such as the stereoscope, had contributed to the challenge to monocularity. Commercially distributed in the 1840s, the stereoscope, as mentioned earlier,

questioned a single, unified point of view. For it demonstrated how seeing was actually the brain's combining of what our eyes see slightly differently. Only in the stereoscope with mirrors, or later, lenses, could one view two photographs of the same scene or figure, accommodating different angles of vision, and get a partial depth of field. In addition, art photographers well before the 1880s or 1890s were already experimenting in ways that would alter the relationship of the observer to the image by manipulation of the print, the relationship of figure and ground, borders, lines, and figure placement within the frame, and issues of focus.

7. Twenty years before Edouard Manet, Robinson is intrigued with fixing and holding elements of a picture in place that keep threatening to drift off. According to Crary, "Manet's *In the Conservatory* is . . . an attempt to reconsolidate a visual field that was in many ways being disassembled" (1995, 53); see Fried.

8. Hawarden might have found an admirer in Jacques Lacan, who contrasts tactile visuality that is obvious even to a blind man and "optical visuality or 'atmospheric surround' in which the viewer, no longer a surveyor, is 'caught within the onrush of light'" (Krauss 33, as quoted in Iverson 1994, 461). He writes: "Light may travel in a straight line, but it is refracted, diffused, it floods, it fills—the eye is a sort of bowl—it flows over too . . . " (94). Glass and steel enclosures of the mid-Victorian period, like the Crystal Palace which let in "unprecedented amounts of light," have notably been cited as a source of the Impressionist challenge to Cartesian perspectivalism (Jay 1993, 124, citing Schievelbusch; and see I. Armstrong 2008).

9. Handy 3–4; Lukacher in Handy 42.

10. Rejlander 76–78. In 1857, over about six weeks, Rejlander created his most famous work, "The Two Ways of Life," now in the collection of the Royal Photographic Society, a montaged print made from thirty-two negatives. Another photograph from the same year was his still disconcerting "The Head of John the Baptist in a Charger," which appears to be a head floating in a basin, begun as part of a larger project concerning Salomé. In the 1860s, Rejlander experimented with double exposure, photographs of dreams, photomontage, and retouching. He was widely known in Britain and abroad through lecturing, publishing, and duplicates of his work, sold by book and art dealers.

11. Trained as an apprentice from the age of thirteen in all aspects of printing and engraving (Harker 6), Robinson found mentors, read Ruskin, visited and memorized the works in the National Gallery, and embarked on painting. Soon after, though, Robinson turned to the new and exciting medium of photography. He opened his first studio in Leamington Spa in 1857.

12. J. Smith 2006 notes that Rejlander in the 1860s became best known for his expression studies, promoting photography as a better medium for capturing expression than painting (217). No doubt it was this point of view that led Darwin to choose Rejlander as one of his illustrators for *The Expression of the Emotions in Man and Animals* (1872).

13. Though he had assistants put the prints together, Robinson was not careless and worked hard over the years to improve his technique to eliminate any lines or blank spaces. In one of his numerous books on his craft, *Pictorial Effect in Photography being Hints on Composition and Chiaroscuro for Photographers* (1869), for instance, he offers suggestions for diminishing the evidence of the "joins": "If great care be taken to print both plates exactly alike in depth, it will be impossible to

discover the join in the finished print" (194); "When printed the picture should be carefully examined, to see if the joins may be improved or be made less visible. It will be found that, in many places, the effect can be improved and the junctions made more perfect, especially where a light comes against a dark—such as a distant landscape against the dark part of a dress—by tearing away the edge of the mask covering the dark, and supplying its place by touches of black varnish at the back of the negative; this, in printing, will cause the lines to be less defined, and the edges to soften into each other" (195): "In making a photograph of a large group, as many figures as possible should be obtained in each negative, and the position of the joins so contrived that they shall come in places where they will be least noticed, if seen at all" (196).

14. Critical attention has come to Hawarden late, in part because her photographs were donated to the Victoria and Albert Museum, London, by her family only in 1939 and in part because she was an amateur. Since the 1980s, Hawarden's photographic subject matter and technical brilliance have drawn critical notice, particularly by women. Virginia Dodier is responsible for compiling the catalogue raisonné of the 775 photographs held by the Victoria and Albert Museum.

15. See http://query.nytimes.com/gst/fullpage.html?res=9C0CE3D8173AF934 A15754C0A966958260.
Downloaded January 9, 2007.

16. Hawarden was highly favorably reviewed in terms of her technique. A review of her first show with the Photographic Society in *Photographic News* 7, no. 244 (February 27, 1863): 99 remarks on a highly bromized collodion and Dallmeyer's No. 1 Triple lens that ensures the "wondrous depth of definition" (Dodier 1999, 12). In 1864 the *Photographic News* lauds her works as "unrivalled" and "surpassed by nothing in the exhibition." *The Photographic News* 8, no. 303 (June 24): 30 (see Ramirez 4).

17. Whether or not the Victorians experienced or recognized Hawarden's work as "about adolescence," since the psychosocial category as such was not in currency "until some thirty years later," is an interesting question (Silver 83). If one understands cultural moments as harboring emergent categories, however, one could suggest that Hawarden helped to instantiate the very concept of adolescence, whether named or not.

18. Julie Codell suggests that Hawarden's photos "fit Victorian social and class eroticisms by providing images of the poor, the peasant, the child, the chivalric hero, and the damsel in distress" (479).

19. Aileen Tsui interprets Whistler's "tactical deployment" of multiple titling of *The Little White Girl* (1862) "to bait and then counter the public's taste for narrative painting" as part of his aesthetic purism and rage against ignorant critics (447).

20. While both eroticize girls, Carroll is interested in fixing prepubescent girls at an age of innocence. He affixes a photograph of Alice to "Alice's Adventures Under Ground," which would become *Alice in Wonderland* (1865). Hawarden, in contrast, photographs the transitions and blurrings of what we call adolescence, rather than arresting childhood or bemoaning/preventing achievements of maturity.

21. Carol Mavor importantly notes that Hawarden effects "an everlasting process of reduplication between mother and child, between stereoscopic images" (45). She suggests that Hawarden's use of mirrors is not only in the service of "female

narcissism but the mirroring of the mother through the daughters." She goes on (38ff) to argue for a reading of props, such as vases or shells or pearls, as fetishistic objects that simulate Hawarden's and her daughters' bodies. It seems to me that Hawarden is extremely concerned with line and shape. She piles on drapery to create forms. She selects objects that mirror or invert shapes of her daughters' bodies, skirts, hair, and thus makes the photographs pulsate with a kind of reduplicated physicality, but my reading is not concerned with "women as ontologically fetishistic" (40). Criticized for her overly subjective responses to Hawarden, Mavor yet fastens on something essential to the work, as she draws attention both to the erotic and to the more traditional representations of Victorian girls which, in her view, address the crisis of the in-between state of the age of consent. See Silver; Codell; and Haworth-Booth for comments on Mavor's interpretations.

22. To add to the allure of the collection, as Dodier reports (1999, 11), Hawarden did not leave many letters or a journal, she does not appear much in the written record, and her photographs were originally undated and untitled. The fact that the photographs were torn out of albums adds to their allure, but it also alters the size and shape of the prints, adding to the repeated trope we find in criticism of Hawarden: that the pictures are mysterious, that our suppositions can be only speculative, and that the images are open for multiple interpretations (see Mavor; Dodier 1991 and 1999; Warner; and Rose 2000 and 2002, for example).

23. Craig Owens reminds us that in the nineteenth century there is an analogical relationship between photograph and mirror. As early as 1839, he reports, Jules Janin, introducing photography, urged readers to "imagine that the mirror has retained the imprint of every object it reflects, then you will have a more complete idea of the Daguerreotype" (Owens 75, fn. 1)

24. Lady Hawarden, whose mother was a Spanish Roman Catholic, would have understood Marian symbology. In one later set of photographs, Hawarden captures Clementina wearing a star at her forehead and a Roman-style dress, as if she were Venus. In comparison to a nun-figure in another of the photographs, perhaps she represents, in her costume, a lusting Venus. Surely the contradiction—Clementina as virgin, Clementina as goddess of love—is the point. Both aspects of femininity are alive and often at odds during adolescence.

25. It is also important to remember that photographed tableaux were connected with the instruction of children. See Lukacher in Handy 31, where he cites George Bernard Shaw's 1883 "wry prospectus for the future of photography" in his novel *An Unsocial Socialist*: "Historical pictures replaced by photography of *tableaux vivants* formed and arranged by actors and artists, and used chiefly for the instruction of children. Nine-tenths of painting as we understand it at present extinguished by the completion of these photographs." While I do not see Hawarden as posing her children to then instruct them with prints of themselves, I do see her as using the process of posing and dressing up, itself, as a form of instruction, not only as an imaginative escape but also in cultural narratives and rituals of romance, female independence, and female identity.

26. The mirror in art history has a long and distinguished history, particularly paired with the female figure in Western and Eastern traditions, and it is known that Hawarden visited the art galleries in Rome and Florence in 1841–42, as well as in London (Dodier 1999, 17). It is likely that she was schooled in Italian and other European art.

27. One can't help but think of the many examples of children's literature, early nineteenth-century instances of which Hawarden's daughters may have heard read aloud or read to each other, in which alternate realities or parallel universes lie behind a wall, a curtain, a mirror, or a layer like skin or in which figures emerge from them. Some of the more prominent later examples include: Jean Ingelow's *Mopsa the Fairy* (1869), Carroll's *Through the Looking Glass and What Alice Found There* (1871), Mary Louisa Molesworth's *The Tapestry Room* (1879), and Frances Hodgson Burnett's "Behind the White Brick" (1881). Modern examples continue this tradition: C. S. Lewis's *The Chronicles of Narnia* (1949–54), Philip Pullman's *The Golden Compass* (1995), and many more. This is a common trope in poetry of the nineteenth century as well, the most important, oft-cited, and photographically interpreted example (Robinson's "Sleep") being Matthew Arnold's "Tristram and Iseult" (1852) in which a tapestry of a medieval warrior comes alive in Tristram's room and the figure comments on the scene.

28. Bryan J. Wolf's discussion of *Woman with a Pearl Necklace* (1664) by Vermeer has influenced my thinking about Hawarden's photograph of Clementina in profile. Although Carol Mavor connects Hawarden with Vermeer and Dutch realism, my interest is independence; my argument is governed by the work of scholars of perspective such as Elkins (1994, 1996, 2005) and Grootenboer and by the close readings and research of Wolf.

29. Jette Kjeldsen reports that when Swinburne's poem "Before the Mirror," inspired by Whistler's *The Little White Girl*, was exhibited in London at the Royal Academy in 1865 with the "poem printed on gold paper and pasted to the frame" (87), Whistler was delighted with Swinburne's "correspondence of mood and atmosphere rather than of specific content" (87–88). Also see 120n2. On Picasso, see Kimmelman and Grundberg (1986).

CHAPTER 4

1. During the nineteenth century, painting remained the art most frequently compared to literature, though the function of the analogy altered. In the early modern period, painting was elevated over literature. This hierarchy gradually reversed itself. See Hagstrum all and Witemeyer (34). In the twentieth century, narrative theory in confronting vision and language offered increasingly refined explanations of objective knowledge and the subject. See Bal 1996, 170–71 and Damisch.

2. For criticism of the novel and omniscience, besides essays on specific narrators, see Jaffe; Freedman; and Buzard.

3. Miller (1963) and Beer approached nineteenth-century literature in terms of its relationship to the "disappearance of God" and to the rise of scientific theories such as evolution, respectively.

4. For comparisons of realism to Dutch painting or allusions to paintings in fictions or poems, see Yeazell; Bullen; Witemeyer; Andres. For relations of the arts see Mitchell 1977 and Hagstrum.

5. Caroline Levine (2007) also cites Dames for his interventions into formalism.

6. Individual studies of authors and the sophisticated analysis of realism by

Welsh, Knoepflmacher, George Levine, McKeon, and others have led in this direction, but almost all critics of realism have stayed within novel studies and have not
drawn on critical insights from the study of poetry. To appreciate the persistence
of the association of realism with verisimilitude and mimesis, note the influence of
theorists of the novel such as Ian Watt. Michael McKeon puts it this way: "Watt's
argument brings the novelistic aim of empirical objectivity to the forefront, but at
the expense of the self-conscious reflexivity that his predecessors treat as an equal
and obverse effect of the novel's epistemological distance" (356). To illustrate the
size of the problem, though, the reliance among almost all theorists of narrative,
including the highly influential Gérard Genette, on linear teleology, rather than
space, or rather than space-time coordinates, severely limits how we read representation. It perpetuates a temporally driven, realist-based model of interpretation
(see Skordili, Introduction).

7. See J. Hillis Miller (2008; 82).

8. Chandler's summary of the dramatic monologue, derived from Langbaum,
is, however, far too simplistic. While Langbaum takes account of a dual reaction,
he views judgment as a moral disciplining of sympathy.

9. In Smith's *The Theory of Moral Sentiments* (1759), the ongoing practice of
sympathetic identification with an other by an observer establishes bases for judgment. The individual needs to be able to put himself into the position of the other,
whether like or unlike the other, in order to judge neutrally another's reaction to
a situation: "As we have no immediate experience of what other men feel, we can
form no idea of the manner in which they are affected, but by conceiving what
we ourselves should feel in the like situation. . . . It is the impressions of our own
senses only, not those of his, which our imaginations copy. By the imagination,
we place ourselves in his situation." http://www.und.nodak.edu/instruct/wein-
stei/The%20Theory%20of%20Moral%20Sentiments%20by%20Adam%20Smith.
pdf. Downloaded February 10, 2008. See Schor on Adam Smith's designation of
sympathy for the dead as a key stage in the theory of moral sentiments (34–40).

10. The pseudonym of Mary Ann Evans, George Eliot, will be used in full in
each instance, as is customary.

11. For a useful overview of case logic, see Lauren Berlant, "On the Case."

12. See Friedberg 2006, chapter 1.

13. Slinn 1976.

14. Contemporary critics noted the relationship of the novel to the epistolary
mode to claim Collins was not an innovator. Yet J. Taylor explains how the central
voice in *Basil*, for example, is unlike confessional fictional texts before it, such as
those by William Godwin or James Hogg (76–77).

15. See Kucich for a different reading: "One hallmark of Victorian fiction is its
exploration of the conditions in which finessing the truth could be regarded as a
sign of collective social skill and authority" (34).

16. See Pykett 5–6.

17. Kendrick notes that the Preamble was included with Walter Hartright's
testimony after serial publication (24), though most current editions separate it,
including those by Penguin and Broadview. Also see Gaylin 208 n. 10. The Preamble refers to Walter in the third person, which can be taken in two different
ways. It can be read as signifying a different narrator who serves as editor and
introduces Hartright first, or it can be read as Walter's creation of a legal-like

opening to establish the authority of what follows as collected evidence, though, as becomes evident later, he is also an editor. Technically a Preamble introduces a constitution or statute that usually states the reasons for and intent of the law.

18. See Hughes on Collins's relationship to the providential plot of stage melodrama (137). On the providential plot, see Qualls.

19. William Wilkie Collins, named after his father, William Collins, the well-known landscape and genre painter, soon came to be known as Wilkie, after his godfather, the painter David Wilkie. His brother Charles Allston Collins, also a painter, is most famous for the Pre-Raphaelite–inspired canvas *Convent Thoughts*.

20. See Knoepflmacher 1975 on the similarities between Halcombe and Fosco.

21. The basis of "omniscience" seems to be the articulated but loose analogy between God and the author, accompanied by an equally loose analogy between the author and the narrator (the latter clearly untenable, as countless studies have illustrated, but unable to be entirely shaken off). See Culler, who argues we should do away with the term entirely (30–31).

22. For a penetrating study of Eliot's narratorial self-interruptions in the later *Middlemarch*, see Buzard chapter 11. "By the time Eliot writes *Middlemarch*," he suggests, "her narrator appears to recognize herself . . . and to acknowledge herself, as endowed with the Midas-like power to turn virtually any character, however unlikable or merely useful to the plot, into the gold of sympathy-stimulating three-dimensionality" (282). He further suggests "her narrator exhibits consciousness that she could 'enter into' any character . . . and that she 'might' do so, with disastrous consequences" (fn 4).

23. For a useful charting of Eliot's dialogue with Lewes about vision and the imagination, from at least 1859 onward, see Flint 98–116.

24. Regarding Ruskin, Eliot wrote to Barbara Bodichon, "What books his last two are! I think he is the finest living writer" (Eliot, *Letters*, II: 255; Haight 197). She had read the third Volume of *Modern Painters* in 1856 and reviewed it in April of that year. As Witemeyer reports (142), George Eliot first saw examples of Turner's work in 1851 (Eliot, *Letters*, I: 347); she refers to "a Turnerian haze of network" in "Janet's Repentance" and "a faery landscape in Turner's latest style" in *Brother Jacob*. She appears, according to Edward Dowden in 1877, to be under the influence of Turner in constructing the bridge scenes of *Daniel Deronda*. She mentions Turner in relationship to a sunset in a letter to Barbara Bodichon (Eliot, *Letters*, IV: 476) and clearly sees the painter in Ruskinian terms (radical in terms of perspective, moral, and emotional) as going well beyond the picturesque.

25. Miller 1968, Ermarth 1985, Welsh, and Knoepflmacher 1968 are significant exceptions.

26. See George Levine 1980 and Ermarth 1974.

27. Some critics have labeled the Cass plot realistic and the Marner plot a fairy tale and have, by analogy, linked the two men, respectively, with logic and illogic, chance and free will. Alternatively, critics argue for hierarchy. Others suggest that the two perspectives, though in different modes, are progressively integrated partly at the level of narration (Knoepflmacher 1968, 238–39). Kristin Brady suggests the plots are knitted together only at the end. Thale notes that the "two visions, if not reconciled, are at least each given their due" (Thale 68).

28. "ravel." *Online Etymology Dictionary*. Douglas Harper, Historian. June 4, 2007. <Dictionary.com *http://dictionary.reference.com/browse/ravel*>.

29. We are not in the realm of Genesis here, except in a Higher Criticism's version of it. So too Turner's *Light and Colour* (cover art), which George Eliot may well have seen in 1851, invites the eye not to behold Divinity in its rainbows, but to co-create bubbles of light and color while co-writing text. As Carroll definitively shows, each topic of discussion at the Rainbow Inn "centers on the impossibility of discovering absolute standards of judgment" (190).

30. U. C. Knoepflmacher helpfully notes that the name Cass is from *casus* ("fall," as is the case), and Godfrey is a play on God-Free, at peace with God or, ironically, wishing to be free of God (1968, 241). The name also recalls Morris's Godmar, who while acting like a god in determining who lives and who dies, mars one of our most cherished hopes—that the innocent will be spared an unjust, humiliating end.

Agosta, Lucien L. "Animate Images: The Later Poem-Paintings of Dante Gabriel Rossetti." *Texas Studies in Literature and Language* 23 (1981): 78–101.

Alpers, Svetlana. *The Art of Describing: Dutch Art in the Seventeenth Century.* Chicago: University of Chicago Press, 1983.

Ainsworth, Maryan Wynn, ed. *Dante Gabriel Rossetti and the Double Work of Art.* New Haven: Yale Art Gallery, 1976.

Altick, Richard. *Paintings from Books: Art and Literature in Britain, 1760–1900.* Columbus: The Ohio State University Press, 1985.

Andres, Sophia. *The Pre-Raphaelite Art of the Victorian Novel: Narrative Challenges to Visual Gendered Boundaries.* Columbus: The Ohio State University Press, 2005.

Anger, Suzy, ed. *Knowing the Past: Victorian Literature and Culture.* Ithaca: Cornell University Press, 2001.

Armstrong, Carol. "From Clementina to Kasebier: The Photographic Attainment of the 'Lady Amateur.'" *October* (Winter 2000): 101–39.

Armstrong, Isobel. *Language as Living Form in Nineteenth Century Poetry.* Sussex: Harvester, 1982.

———. "'The Lady of Shalott': Optical Elegy" NAVSA. https:www.cla.purdue.edu/English/navsa/documents. Accessed July 20, 2006.

———. *Victorian Glassworlds: Glass Culture and the Imagination 1830–1880.* New York: Oxford University Press, 2008.

———. *Victorian Poetry: Poetry, Poetics, and Politics.* New York: Routledge, 1993.

Armstrong, Nancy. *Fiction in the Age of Photography: The Legacy of British Realism.* Cambridge, MA: Harvard University Press, 1999.

Auerbach, Erich. *Mimesis: The Representation of Reality in Western Literature.* Tr. Willard Trask. New York: Anchor, 1953; orig. German 1942.

Bal, Mieke. *Double Exposures: The Subject of Cultural Analysis.* London: Routledge, 1996.

———. *Narratology: Introduction to the Theory of Narrative.* 2nd ed. Toronto: University of Toronto Press, 1997.

———. *Reading 'Rembrandt': Beyond the Word Image Opposition.* New York: Cambridge University Press, 1991.

135

————. "Visual Essentialism and the Object of Visual Culture." *Journal of Visual Culture* 2.1 (2003): 5–32.

Barlow, Helen Grace. "Truth and Subjectivity: Explorations in Identity and the Real in the Photographic Work of Clementina Hawarden (1822–65), Samuel Butler (1835–1902) and their Contemporaries." PhD Dissertation, University of Kent, Canterbury. 1994.

Barringer, Tim. *Reading the Pre-Raphaelites.* New Haven: Yale University Press, 1998.

Barthes, Roland. "The Reality Effect." In *French Literary Theory Today: A Reader.* Ed. Tzvetan Todorov; trans. R. Carter, 1–17. Cambridge: Cambridge University Press, 1982.

Beer, Gillian. *Darwin's Plots.* New York: Ark, 1985; orig. 1983.

Benjamin, Walter. *Illuminations.* Trans. Harry Zohn; ed. Hannah Arendt. New York: Schocken, 1969.

Berlant, Lauren. "On the Case." *Critical Inquiry* 33.4 (Summer 2007): 633–72.

Bhabha, Homi. "Signs Taken for Wonders." In *The Location of Culture,* 102–22. New York: Routledge, 1994.

Brady, Kristin. *George Eliot.* London: Macmillan, 1992.

Brantlinger, Patrick. "What Is 'Sensational' about the 'Sensation Novel'?" *Nineteenth-Century Fiction* 37.1 (1982): 1–28.

Brooks, Chris. *Signs for the Times: Symbolic Realism in the Mid-Victorian World.* London: George, Allen, & Unwin, 1984.

Browning, Robert. "Introductory Essay." *Letters of Percy Bysshe Shelley.* London: Moxon, 1852.

————. *The Poetical Works of Robert Browning.* Ed. Ian Jack and Margaret Smith. Oxford: Clarendon, volumes 1–9, 1983–.

Bryson, Norman. *Vision and Painting: The Logic of the Gaze.* New Haven: Yale University Press, 1983.

Bullen, J. B. *The Expressive Eye: Fiction and Perception in the Work of Thomas Hardy.* Oxford: Clarendon, 1986.

Burgin, Victor. "Introduction." *Thinking Photography.* London: Macmillan, 1982.

Buzard, James. *Disorienting Fiction: The Autoethnographic Work of Nineteenth-Century British Novels.* Princeton: Princeton University Press, 2005.

Byerly, Alison. *Realism, Representation, and the Arts in Nineteenth-Century Literature.* Cambridge: Cambridge University Press, 1997.

Carlyle, Thomas. *Past and Present.* 1843. London: Chapman and Hall, 1872.

Carroll, David. "Reversing the Oracles of Religion." In *Literary Monographs 1.* Ed. Erich Rothstein and Thomas K. Dunseath, 175–81. Madison: University of Wisconsin Press, 1967.

Catalogue of the Association for Promoting the Free Exhibition of Modern Art. London: Gallery, Hyde Park Corner, 1849.

Cavell, Stanley. "'Photograph, Screen, and Star.'" In *The Cavell Reader.* Ed. Stephen Mullhall, 156–66. London: Blackwell, 1996.

Chandler, James. "On the Face of the Case: Conrad, *Lord Jim,* and the Sentimental Novel." *Critical Inquiry* 33.4 (Summer 2007): 837–64.

Christ, Carol T., and John O. Jordan, eds. *The Victorians and the Visual Imagination.* Berkeley: University of California Press, 1995.

Codell, Julie. "Review of Mavor and Dodier." *Biography* 24.2 (Spring 2001): 477–84.

Cohan, Steven, and Linda M. Shires. *Telling Stories: A Theoretical Analysis of Narrative Fiction*. New York: Routledge, 1988.

Coleridge, Samuel Taylor. *The Collected Works of Samuel Taylor Coleridge*. Ed. James Engel and W. Jackson Bate. Volume 7: *Biographica Literaria*. London: Routledge and Kegan Paul Ltd., 1983.

Collins, Wilkie. *Basil*. New York: Dover Publications, 1980.

———. *The Woman in White*. Ed. Maria K. Bachman and Don Richard Cox. Peterborough, Ontario: Broadview, 2006.

———. *The Woman in White*. Ed. Julian Symons. New York: Penguin, 1982.

Cramer, Maurice Browning. "What Browning's Literary Reputation Owed to the Pre-Raphaelites." *ELH* 8.4 (December 1941): 305–21.

Crary, Jonathan. "Nineteenth–Century Visual Incapacities." In *Visual Literacy*. Ed. James Elkins, 59–76. New York: Routledge, 2008.

———. *Suspensions of Perception: Attention, Spectacle, and Modern Culture*. Cambridge: MIT Press, 2001.

———. *Techniques of the Observer: On Vision and Modernity in the Nineteenth Century*. Cambridge, MA: MIT Press, 1992.

———. "Unbinding Vision: Manet and the Attentive Observer in Late Nineteenth Century." In *Cinema and the Invention of Modern Life*. Ed. Leo Charney and Vanessa R. Schwartz, 46–71. Berkeley: University of California Press, 1995.

Cross, J. W., ed. *George Eliot's Life as Related in her Letters and Journals*. 3 vols. Edinburgh: William Blackwood and Sons, 1885.

Culler, Jonathan. "Omniscience." *Narrative* 12.1 (2004): 22–34.

Cvetkovich, Ann. "Ghostlier Determinations: The Economy of Sensation and *The Woman in White*." *Novel* 23 (Autumn 1989): 24–43.

Dames, Nicholas. "Wave-Theories and Affective Physiologies: The Cognitive Strain in Victorian Novel Theories." *Victorian Studies* 46 (Winter 2004): 206–16.

Damisch, Hubert. *The Origin of Perspective*. Trans. John Goodman. Cambridge. MA: MIT Press, 1995. Original French edition 1987.

Daston, Lorraine, and Peter Galison. "The Image of Objectivity." *Representations* 40, Special Issue: Seeing Science (Autumn 1992): 81–128.

Davis, Michael. *George Eliot and Nineteenth-Century Psychology: Exploring the Unmapped Country*. Burlington, VT: Ashgate, 2006.

Debord, Guy. *The Society of the Spectacle*. New York: Zone, 1995.

Descartes, René. *Selected Philosophical Writings*. Ed. John Cottingham, Robert Stoothoff, and Dugald Murdoch. Cambridge: Cambridge University Press, 1988.

Dickens, Charles. *Sketches by Boz*. 1836. New York: Penguin, 1996.

Didi-Huberman, Georges. *Confronting Images: Questioning the Ends of a Certain History of Art*. Trans. John Goodman. University Park: Pennsylvania State University Press, 2005.

Doane, Mary Ann. *The Desire to Desire: The Woman's Film of the 1940s*. Bloomington: Indiana University Press, 1987.

Dodier, Virginia. "From the Interior: Photographs by Clementina, Viscountess Hawarden." *Magazine Antiques* 139.1 (January 1991): 196–207.

———. *Lady Hawarden. Studies from Life, 1857–1864*. Introduction by Marina Warner. Afterword by Mark Haworth-Booth. New York: Aperture, 1999.

Doughty, Oswald. *A Victorian Romantic: Dante Gabriel Rossetti*. New Haven: Yale

University Press, 1960.

Doughty, Oswald, and J. R. Wahl. *The Letters of Dante Gabriel Rossetti.* 4 vols. Oxford: Oxford University Press, 1965–1967.

Douma, Michael. Curator. Color Vision and Art 2006. "Turner and Delacroix" Web Exhibits. Institute for Dynamic Educational Advancement, Washington, D.C. Downloaded May 1, 2006. http:www.webexhibites.org/colorart/romantic-color.html.

Drucker, Johanna, and Jerome McGann. "Images as the Text: Pictographs and Pictographic Logic." http://jefferson.village.virginia.edu/~jjm2f/old/pictograph.html. Downloaded June 23, 2008.

Eliot, George. *Essays of George Eliot.* Ed. Thomas Pinney. London: Routledge and Kegan Paul, 1963.

———. *The George Eliot Letters.* Vols. 1–9, 1840–1870. Ed. Gordon S. Haight. New Haven: Yale University Press, 1954–1978.

———. *Middlemarch.* Ed. Gordon Haight. Boston: Houghton Mifflin, 1956.

———. *Silas Marner: The Weaver of Raveloe.* Ed. Q. D. Leavis. New York: Penguin, 1967.

Elkins, James. "The End of the Theory of the Gaze." From a work in progress. Revised October 2005. "The Visual How It Is Studied." http://www.jameselkins.com/Texts/visualculturegaze.pdf. Downloaded January 13, 2009.

———. "A Multicultural Look at Space and Form," from a work in progress. Revised October 2005. http://james elkins and Texts/space and form.pdf Down loaded January 13, 2009.

———. *The Object Stares Back: On the Nature of Seeing.* New York: Harcourt Brace, 1996.

———. *The Poetics of Perspective.* Ithaca: Cornell University Press, 1994.

Ermarth, Elizabeth Deeds. *George Eliot.* Boston: Twayne, 1985.

———. "Incarnations: George Eliot's Conception of 'Undeviating Law.'" *Nineteenth Century Fiction* 29 (1974): 273–86.

Faxon, Alice Craig. *Dante Gabriel Rossetti.* New York: Abbeville, 1989.

Ferguson, George. *Signs and Symbols in Christian Art, with Illustrations of Paintings from the Renaissance.* New York: Oxford University Press, 1954.

Finch, Casey, and Peter Bowen. "The Solitary Companionship of *L'Allegro* and *Il Penseroso.*" *Milton Studies* 26 (1990): 3–24.

Fish, Thomas E. "'Action in Character': The Epiphanies of *Pippa Passes.*" *SEL* 25.4 (Autumn 1985): 845–64.

Flint, Kate. *The Victorians and the Visual Imagination.* New York: Oxford University Press, 2000.

Foucault, Michel. *Discipline & Punish: The Birth of the Prison.* New York: Pantheon, 1978.

Fredeman, William E. "The Pre-Raphaelite Literary-Art of Dante Gabriel Rossetti." *Journal of Pre-Raphaelite and Aesthetic Studies* 1.2 (Fall 1988): 54–74.

Freedman, Jonathan. *Professions of Taste: Henry James, British Aestheticism, and Commodity Culture.* Palo Alto: Stanford University Press, 1993.

Fried, Michael. *Manet's Modernism: or, The Face of Painting in the 1860s.* Chicago: University of Chicago Press, 1995.

Friedberg, Anne. *The Virtual Window from Alberti to Microsoft.* Cambridge, MA: MIT Press, 2006.

———. *Window Shopping: Cinema and the Postmodern.* Berkeley: University of California Press, 1993.

Frye, Northrup. *Fearful Symmetry: A Study of William Blake*. 10th printing. Princeton: Princeton University Press, 1990. Originally published 1947.

Fuss, Diana. "Look Who's Talking, or If Looks Could Kill." *Critical Inquiry* 22.2 (Winter 1996): 383–92.

Garrett, Marvin P. "Language and Design in 'Pippa Passes.'" *Victorian Poetry* 13 (1975): 47–60.

Gaylin, Ann. *Eavesdropping in the Novel from Austen to Proust*. Cambridge: Cambridge University Press, 2002.

Glanville, Helen. "Contemporary Colour Theory." In *Pre Raphaelite Painting Technique*, 29–38. London: Tate, 2004.

Goethe, Johan Wolfgang von. *Goethe's Theory of Colours*. Trans. Charles Lock Eastlake. London: John Murray, 1840.

Green-Lewis, Jennifer. *Framing the Victorians: Photography and the Culture of Realism*. Ithaca: Cornell University Press, 1996.

Groth, Helen. *Victorian Photography and Literary Nostalgia*. Oxford: Oxford University Press, 2003.

Grootenboer, Hanneke. *The Rhetoric of Perspective: Realism and Illusionism in Seventeenth Century Still Life Painting*. Chicago: University of Chicago Press, 2005.

Grundberg, Andy. "Photography View: When Picasso Used Film for a Palette." *The New York Times*, May 25, 1986. http://query.nytimes.com. Downloaded January 9, 2007.

———. Review/Photography. "Victorian Mothers' Daughters: So Pure, So Romantic." *The New York Times*, July 17, 1990. http://query.nytimes.com. Downloaded January 9, 2007.

Guillén, Claudio. *Literature as System; Essays toward the Theory of Literary History*. Princeton: Princeton University Press, 1971.

Gunning, Tom. "Review: *Techniques of the Observer On Visions and Modernity in the Nineteenth Century*." *Film Quarterly* 46.1 (Autumn 1992): 51–53.

Hagstrum, Jean. *The Sister Arts; the Tradition of Literary Pictorialism and English Poetry from Dryden to Gray*. Chicago: University of Chicago Press, 1958.

Hair, Donald. *Browning's Experiments in Genre*. Toronto: University of Toronto Press, 1972.

Hallam, Arthur Henry. "On Some of the Characteristics of Modern Poetry." In *Victorian Poetry and Poetics*. Ed. Walker E. Houghton and G. Robert Stange, 848–60. New York: Houghton Mifflin Company, 1968.

Handy, Ellen, ed. and Curator. *Photographs and Theories of Henry Peach Robinson and Peter Henry Emerson*. Norfolk, VA: Chrysler Museum, 1994.

Hardy, Florence Emily. *The Early Life of Thomas Hardy 1840–1891*. London: Macmillan, 1928.

Harker, Margaret F. *Henry Peach Robinson: Master of Photographic Art, 1830–1901*. London: Blackwell, 1988.

Hartman, Anne. "Doing Things with Poems: Performativity and Cultural Form." *Victorian Poetry* 41.4 (Winter 2003): 481–90.

Haworth-Booth, Mark. "The Return of Lady Hawarden." In *Lady Hawarden, Studies From Life 1857–1864*, by Virginia Dodier, 110–15. New York: Aperture, 1999.

Heller, Tamar. *Dead Secrets: Wilkie Collins and the Female Gothic*. New Haven: Yale University Press, 1992.

Helmholtz, Hermann von. *Treatise on Physiological Optics*. Trans. James P. C.

Southlall. New York: Dover, 1962.

Helsinger, Elizabeth. "William Morris before Kelmscott, Poetry and Design in the 1860s." In *The Victorian Illustrated Book.* Ed. Richard Maxwell, 209–38. Charlottesville: University of Virginia Press, 2002.

Hewitt, Martin. "Why the Notion of Victorian Britain *Does* Make Sense." *Victorian Studies* 48.3 (Spring 2006): 395–438.

Heyert, Elizabeth. *The Glass House Years: Victorian Portrait Photography 1839–1870.* Montclair, NJ: Allanheld and Schram, 1979.

Houghton, Walter E., and G. Robert Stange. *Victorian Poetry and Poetics.* New York: Houghton Mifflin Company, 1968.

Hughes, Winifred. *The Maniac in the Cellar: the Sensation Novel of the 1860s.* Princeton: Princeton University Press, 1980.

Irigaray, Luce. *Speculum of the Other Woman.* Ithaca: Cornell University Press, 1985.

Iverson, Margaret. "The Discourse of Perspective in the Twentieth Century: Panofsky, Damisch, Lacan." *Oxford Art Journal* 28.2 (June 2005): 191–202. *http://oaj. oxford journals.org/cgi/content/full/28/2/191* 1–14. Downloaded June 13, 2008.

———. "What Is a Photograph?" *Art History* 17.3 (September 1994): 450–64.

Jaffe, Audrey. *Vanishing Points: Dickens, Narrative, and the Subject of Omniscience.* Berkeley: University of California Press, 1991.

Jay, Martin. "Cultural Relativism and the Visual Turn." *Journal of Visual Culture* 1.2 (2003): 267–78.

———. *Downcast Eyes, the Denigration of Vision in Twentieth-Century French Thought.* Berkeley: University of California Press, 1993.

———. "Modernism and the Specter of Psychologism." *Modernism/Modernity* 3.2 (1996): 93–111.

Jenks, Christopher. *Visual Culture.* London: Routledge, 1995.

Johnson, E. D. H. *The Alien Vision of Victorian Poetry: Sources of the Poetic Imagination in Tennyson, Browning, and Arnold.* Princeton: Princeton University Press, 1952.

Keats, John. *Complete Poems.* Ed. Jack Stillinger. Cambridge, MA: Belknap Press of Harvard University Press, 1991.

Kemp, Martin. *The Science of Art: Optical Themes in Western Art from Brunelleschi to Seurat.* New Haven: Yale University Press, 1990.

Kendrick, Walter. "The Sensationalism of *The Woman in White.*" *Nineteenth-Century Fiction* 32.1 (June 1977): 18–35.

Kimmelman, Michael. "Art View: Photographs That Fed Picasso's Vision." *The New York Times.* January 11, 1998. http://query.nytimes.com. Dowloaded November 4, 2006.

King, Roma. *The Focusing Artifice: the Poetry of Robert Browning.* Athens: Ohio University Press, 1968.

Kjeldsen, Jette. "What Can the Aesthetic Movement Tell Us about Aesthetic Education." *Journal of Aesthetic Education* 35.1 (Spring 2001): 85–97.

Knoepflmacher, U. C. *George Eliot's Early Novels: The Limits of Realism.* Berkeley: University of California Press, 1968.

———. "The Counterworld of Victorian Fiction and *The Woman in White.*" *Worlds of Victorian Fiction.* Ed. Jerome H. Buckley. Cambridge., MA: Harvard University Press, 1975.

Korg, Jacob. "'A Reading of Pippa Passes.'" *Victorian Poetry* 6.1 (1968): 5–19.

Kramer, Dale. "Character and Theme in 'Pippa Passes.'" *Victorian Poetry* 2.4 (1964):

241–49.

Krasner, James. *The Entangled Eye: Visual Perception and the Representation of Nature in Post-Darwinian Narrative*. New York: Oxford University Press, 1992.

Krauss, Rosalind. *The Optical Unconscious*. Cambridge, MA: MIT Press, 1993.

Kucich, John. *The Power of Lies: Transgression in Victorian Fiction*. Ithaca: Cornell University Press, 1994.

Lacan, Jacques. *The Four Fundamental Concepts of Psychoanalysis*. Ed. Jacques-Alain Miller. New York: Norton, 1998.

Lalvani, Suren. "Photography, Epistemology and the Body." *Cultural Studies* 7.3 (October 1993): 442–65.

Landow, George. "The Finding of the Savior in the Temple." Chapter 2, "Typological Symbolism in Hunt's Major Works." *Replete with Meaning: Holman Hunt and Typological Symbolism*. http://www.victorianweb.org/painting/whh/replete/finding1.html. Accessed January 15, 2009.

———. "Moses Striking the Rock: Typological Symbolism in Victorian Poetry." In *Literary Uses of Typology*. Ed. Earl Miner, 315–44. Princeton: Princeton University Press, 1977.

Langbaum, Robert. *The Poetry of Experience: The Dramatic Monologue in Modern Literary Tradition*. Chicago: University of Chicago Press, 1986; orig. Random House 1957.

Lawson, Julie. *Women in White, Photographs by Lady Hawarden*. Edinburgh: Scottish National Portrait Gallery, 1997.

Lejeune, Philippe. "Autobiography in the Third Person." *New Literary History* 9.1 (Winter 1977): 27–50.

Levine, Caroline. "Formal Pasts and Formal Possibilities in Victorian Studies." *Literature Compass* 5 (2007): 1–16.

———. "Structural Formalism: Toward a New Method in Cultural Studies." *Victorian Studies* 48.4 (Summer 2006): 625–58.

Levine, George. "George Eliot's Hypothesis of Reality." *Nineteenth Century Fiction* 35.1 (June 1980): 1–28.

———. *The Realistic Imagination: English Fiction from Frankenstein to Lady Chatterley*. Chicago: University of Chicago Press, 1983.

Lewes, George Henry. *The Physiology of Common Life*. 2 vols. Edinburgh and London: William Blackwood and Sons, 1859–60.

Lindsay, Jack. *Turner: His Life and Work*. New York: Granada Publishing, 1981.

Loesberg, Jonathan. *Victorialist listserv*. Indiana University. Posted October 10, 2003. Accessed January 13, 2009.

Lonoff, Sue. *Wilkie Collins and His Victorian Readers: A Study in the Rhetoric of Authorship*. New York: AMS Press, 1982.

Lukacher, Brian. "Powers of Sight: Robinson, Emerson, and the Polemics of Pictorial Photography." In Handy 29–53.

Malinowski, Bronislaw. "Myth in Primitive Psychology." In *Magic, Science and Religion and Other Essays*. Boston: Beacon Press, 1948.

Marin, Louis. *On Representation*. Trans. Catherine Porter. Stanford: Stanford University Press, 2001; French original edition, Paris: Sueil/Gallimard, 1994.

Marsh, Jan. *The Pre-Raphaelites: Their Lives in Diaries and Letters*. London: Collins and Brown, 1966.

Martin, Loy D. *Browning's Dramatic Monologues and the Post-Romantic Subject*. Baltimore: Johns Hopkins Press, 1985.

Massey, Lyle. "Anamorphosis through Descartes or Perspective Gone Awry." *Renaissance Quarterly* 50.4 (Winter 1977): 1148–90.

Mavor, Carol. *Becoming: The Photographs of Clementina, Viscountess Hawarden*. Durham: Duke University Press, 1999.

McCarthy, Anna. *Ambient Television: Visual Culture and Public Space*. Durham: Duke University Press, 2001.

McGann, Jerome. "An Introduction to D. G. Rossetti." The Rossetti Archive. http://www.rossettiarchive.org/racs/bio-exhibit/1.html, 1–6. Downloaded January 23, 2007.

———. *Dante Gabriel Rossetti and the Game that Must Be Lost*. New Haven: Yale University Press, 2000.

———. "Medieval versus Victorian versus Modern: Rossetti's Art of Images." *Modernism/modernity* 2.1 (January 1995): 97–112.

McKeon, Michael, ed. *Theory of the Novel: An Historical Approach. A Critical Anthology*. Baltimore: Johns Hopkins University Press, 2000.

Meisel, Martin. *Realizations, Narrative, Pictorial, and Theatrical Arts in Nineteenth Century England*. Princeton: Princeton University Press, 1983.

Melville, Stephen. "Shifting in the Ruins." *Journal of Visual Culture* 4.3 (2005): 275–86.

———. "The Temptation of New Perspectives." *October* 52 (Spring 1990): 3–15.

Merleau-Ponty, Maurice. "Cézanne's Doubt." In *Sense and Non-sense*. Trans. Patricia Allen Dreyfus, 9–25. Evanston, IL: Northwestern University Press, 1992.

———. *The Primacy of Perception and Other Essays on Phenomenological Psychology, the Philosophy of Art, History and Politics*. Evanston, IL: Northwestern University Press, 1964.

Meyers, Jeffrey. *Painting and the Novel*. Manchester: Manchester University Press, 1975.

Miller, J. Hillis. *The Disappearance of God: Five Nineteenth-Century Writers*. Cambridge, MA: Harvard University Press, 1963.

———. *The Forms of Victorian Fiction*. Notre Dame: University of Notre Dame Press, 1968.

———. *Illustration (Essays in Art and Culture)*. Cambridge, MA: Harvard University Press, 1992.

———. "The Mirror's Secret: Dante Gabriel Rossetti's Double Work of Art." *Victorian Poetry* 28.4 (Winter 1991): 335–56.

———. "What Do Stories about Pictures Want?" *Critical Inquiry* 34 (Winter 2008): 59–97.

Milton, John. *Paradise Lost*. Ed. Gordon Teskey. New York: W. W. Norton & Company, 2005.

Mirzoeff, Nicholas. *An Introduction to Visual Culture*. New York: Routledge, 1999.

———. *The Visual Culture Reader*. New York: Routldege, 1998.

Mitchell, W. J. T. *Blake's Composite Art: A Study of the Illuminated Poetry*. Princeton: Princeton University Press, 1977.

———. *Iconology: Image, Text, Ideology*. Chicago: University of Chicago Press, 1986.

———. *Picture Theory: Essays on Visual and Verbal Representation*. Chicago: University of Chicago Press, 1994.

Morris, William. *The Defense of Guinevere and Other Poems*. London: Bell and Daldy,

1858.

———. "Shadows of Amiens." In *The Hollow Land and Other Contributions to the Oxford and Cambridge Magazine.* Ed. Eugene D. LeMire, 289–316. Bristol: Thoemmes Press, 1996.

Moxley, Keith. "Perspective, Panofsky, and the Philosophy of History." *New Literary History* 26.4 (1995): 775–86.

Mulvey, Laura. "Visual Pleasure and Narrative Cinema." *Visual and Other Pleasures.* Basingstoke: Macmillan, 1989.

Nead, Linda. "Velocities of the Image c 1900." *Art History* 27.5 (November 2004): 745–69.

Nochlin, Linda. "Lost and Found: Once More the Fallen Woman. "*Art Bulletin 60* (March 1978): 139–53. Reprinted in *Women, Art, and Power, and Other Essays.* Boulder: Westview, 1989.

Nord, Deborah Epstein. "Rambling in the Nineteenth Century." In *Walking the Victorian Streets: Women, Representation and the City.* Introduction, 1–18. Ithaca: Cornell University Press, 1995.

Owens, Craig. "Photography 'en abyme.'" *October* 5 (Summer 1978): 73–88.

Panofsky, Erwin. *Perspective as Symbolic Form.* New York: Zone 1997; orig. Leipzig/ Berlin: Vorträge der Bibliothek Warburg, 1927.

Pater, Walter. "Dante Gabriel Rossetti." *Appreciations, with an Essay on Style.* London: Macmillan, 1889.

Paulson, Ronald. "Turner's Graffiti: The Sun and its Glosses." In *Images of Romanticism: Verbal and Visual Affinities.* Ed. Karl Kroeber and William Walling, 167–88. New Haven: Yale University Press, 1978.

"Pensive Image." http://www.janvaneyck.nl/)_2_3_events_info/arc_06_thepensiveimage_symposium.html. Downloaded May 18, 2006.

"perspective." *The American Heritage Dictionary of the English Language.* 4th ed. Houghton Mifflin Company, 2004. Dictionary.com *http://dictionary.reference. com/browse/perspective.* Accessed June 13, 2008.

Pollock, Griselda. *Vision and Difference: Femininity, Feminism and the Histories of Art.* London: Routledge, 1988.

Praz, Mario. *Mnemosyne: The Parallel between Literature and the Visual Arts.* Princeton: Princeton University Press, 1970.

Prendeville, Brendan. "Merleau-Ponty, Realism, and Painting: Psychophysical Space and the Space of Exchange." *Art History* 22.3 (September 1999): 364–88.

Psomiades, Kathy Alexis. *Beauty's Body: Femininity and Representation in British Aestheticism.* Stanford: Stanford University Press, 1997.

Pykett, Lynn. *Wilkie Collins.* New York: Oxford University Press, 2005.

Qualls, Barry. *The Secular Pilgrims of Victorian Fiction.* Cambridge, MA: Harvard University Press, 1982.

Rader, Ralph W. "The Dramatic Monologue and Related Lyric Forms." *Critical Inquiry* 3.1 (Autumn 1976): 131–51.

Ramirez, Jennifer. "On the Double Mirroring and Twinning in the Photographs of Clementina, Lady Hawarden." PhD dissertation, Virginia Commonwealth University, 2003.

Rejlander, Oscar Gustave. "An Apology for Art Photography." *The British Journal of Photography* 10 (February 16, 1863): 76–78.

Ridge, Jacqueline, Joyce H. Townsend, Stephen Hackney, and John Anderson. "The Paintings." In *Pre-Raphaelite Painting Technique, 77–189.* London: Tate, 2004.

Roberts, Russell, with Anthony Burnett-Brown and Michael Gray. *Specimens and Marvels: William Henry Fox Talbot and the Invention of Photography.* New York: Aperture, 2000.

Robinson, Henry Peach. "Composition Not Patchwork." *The British Journal of Photography* 8 (July 2, 1860): 189. http:albumen.stanford.edu/library/c19/robinson2/html. Downloaded April 18, 2006.

———. "On Printing Photographic Pictures from Several Negatives." *The British Journal of Photography* 8 (April 2, 1860: 94. http:albumen.stanford.edu/library/c19/robinson2/html. Downloaded April 18, 2006.

———. *Pictorial Effect in Photography Being Hints on Composition and Chiaroscuro for Photographers.* London: Piper and Carter 1869.

Rooney, Ellen. "Form and Contentment." *Modern Language Quarterly* 61.1 (March 2000): 17–40.

Rose, Gillian. "Practising Photography: An Archive, a Study, Some Photographs and a Researcher." *Journal of Historical Geography* 26.4 (2000): 555–71.

———. *Visual Methodologies.* London: Sage, 2001.

———. "Working on *Women in White*, Again." *Cultural Geographies* 9 (2002): 103–9.

Rossetti Archive. Ed. Jerome McGann. 2006. Institute for Advanced Study in the Humanities. University of Virginia. http://rossettiarchive.org/ Accessed January 13, 2009.

Rossetti, Dante Gabriel. *Collected Poetry and Prose.* Ed. Jerome McGann. New Haven: Yale University Press, 2003.

Ruskin, John. *The Elements of Drawing. The Works of Ruskin.* Vol. 20. Ed. E. T. Cook and Alexander Wedderburn. New York: Longmans, Green and Co., 1904.

———. *The Elements of Perspective. The Works of Ruskin.* Vol. 20. Ed. E. T. Cook and Alexander Wedderburn. New York: Longmans, Green and Co., 1904.

———. *Modern Painters III. The Works of Ruskin.* Vol. 5. Ed. E. T. Cook and Alexander Wedderburn. New York: Longmans, Green and Co., 1904.

———. *Modern Painters V. The Works of Ruskin.* Vol. 7. Ed. E. T. Cook and Alexander Wedderburn. New York: Longmans, Green and Co., 1904.

———. *The Stones of Venice III. The Works of Ruskin.* Vol. 11. Ed. E. T. Cook and Alexander Wedderburn. New York: Longman's Green and Co., 1904.

———. *Turner. The Works of Ruskin.* Vol. 13. Ed. E. T. Cook and Alexander Wedderburn. New York: Longmans, Green and Co., 1904.

Schievelbusch, Wolfgang. *The Railway Journey: The Industrialization of Time and Space in the 19th Century.* Berkeley: University of California Press, 1986.

Schor, Esther. *Bearing the Dead: The British Culture of Mourning from the Enlightenment to Queen Victoria.* Princeton: Princeton University Press, 1994.

Schwartz, Vannessa, and Jeannene M. Przyblyski. *The Nineteenth-Century Visual Culture Reader.* New York: Routledge Press, 2004.

Searle, John R. "*Las Meninas* and the Paradoxes of Pictorial Representation." *Critical Inquiry* 6.3 (Spring 1980): 477–88.

Sekula, Allan. "The Body and the Archive." *October* 39 (Winter 1986): 3–64.

———. "Reading an Archive." *Blasted Allegories,* 114–27. Cambridge, MA: MIT Press, 1987.

Sharp, William. *Dante Gabriel Rossetti. A Record and a Study.* London: Macmillan, 1882.

———. *Life of Browning.* http://www.worldwideschool.org.library/books/. Downloaded August 14, 2006.

Shelley, Percy Bysshe. *Letters of Percy Bysshe Shelley: With an Introductory Essay by Robert Browning*. London: Edward Moxon, 1852.

Shires, Linda M. "The Radical Aesthetic of *Tess of the d'Urbervilles*." In *The Cambridge Companion to Thomas Hardy*. Ed. Dale Kramer, 145–63. Cambridge: Cambridge University Press, 1992.

Shuttleworth, Sally. "Fairy Tale or Science? Physiological Psychology in *Silas Marner*." In *The Languages of Nature: Critical Essays on Science and Literature*. Ed. L. J. Jordanova, 244–88. London: Free Association Books, 1986.

Silver, Carole. Review of Carol Mavor, *Becoming*. *Visual Anthropology Review* 15.1 (Spring/Summer 1999): 83–84.

Skordili, Beatrice. "Destroying Time Topology and Taxonomy in *The Alexandria Quartet*." PhD dissertation, Syracuse University, 2006.

Slinn, E. Warwick. *The Discourse of Self in Victorian Poetry*. New York: Macmillan, 1991.

———. "'God a Tame Confederate': The Reader's Dual Vision in *Pippa Passes*." *UTQ* 45.2 (Winter 1976): 158–72.

———. "Rossetti's Elegy for Masculine Desire: Seduction and Loss in the *House of Life*." In *Haunted Texts: Studies in Pre-Raphaelitism in Honour of William E. Fredeman*. Ed. David Latham, 53–69. Toronto: University of Toronto Press, 2003a.

———. *Victorian Poetry as Cultural Critique: The Politics of Performative Language*. Charlottesville: University of Virginia Press, 2003b.

Smith, Alison. "Revival and Reformation: The Aims and Ideals of the Pre-Raphaelite Brotherhood." In *Pre-Raphaelite Painting Technique*. Ed. Jacqueline Ridge, Joyce H. Townsend, and Stephen Hackney. 9–20. London: Tate, 2004.

Smith, Jonathan. *Charles Darwin and Victorian Visual Culture*. Cambridge: Cambridge University Press, 2006.

Smith, Lindsay. *Victorian Photography, Painting, and Poetry: The Enigma of Visibility in Ruskin, Morris, and the Pre-Raphaelites*. Cambridge: Cambridge University Press, 1995.

Snyder, Joel. "'Las Meninas' and the Mirror of the Prince." *Critical Inquiry* 11.4 (June 1985): 539–72.

Snyder, Joel, and Ted Cohen. "Reflexions on 'Las Meninas': Paradox Lost." *Critical Inquiry* 7.2 (1980): 429–47.

Stein, Richard L. *The Ritual of Interpretation: The Fine Arts as Literature in Ruskin, Rossetti, and Pater*. Cambridge, MA: Harvard University Press, 1975.

Steinberg, Leo. "Velázquez's *Las Meninas*." *October* 19 (Winter 1981): 45–54.

Stephens, F. G. "Mr. Rossetti's New Pictures." *The Athenaeum* (14 April 1877): 486–87.

Surtees, Virginia. *The Paintings and Drawings of Dante Gabriel Rossetti (1828–1882): A Catalogue Raisonné*. Vol. 1. Oxford: Clarendon Press, 1971.

Tagg, John. *The Burden of Representation: Essays on Photographies and Histories*. Amherst: University of Massachusetts Press, 1988.

Talbot, W. H. F. *Some Account of the Art of Photogenic Drawing or the Process by Which Natural Objects May Be Made to Delineate Themselves without the Aid of the Artist's Pencil*. London: R. & J. E. Taylor, 1839.

Taylor, Charles. *Sources of the Self: The Making of Modern Identity*. Cambridge, MA: Harvard University Press, 1989.

Taylor, Jenny Bourne. *In the Secret Theatre of Home: Wilkie Collins, Sensation Narrative, and Nineteenth-Century Psychology.* New York: Routledge, 1988.

Tennyson, Alfred. *The Poems of Tennyson.* Ed. Christopher Ricks. 3 vols. Berkeley: University of California Press, 1969.

Teukolsky, Rachel. "Modernist Ruskin, Victorian Baudelaire: Revisioning Nineteenth Century Aesthetics." *PMLA* 122.3 (May 2007): 711–27.

Thale, Jerome. *The Novels of George Eliot.* New York: Columbia University Press, 1959.

Tinker, Chauncey B. *Painter and Poet: Studies in the Literary Relations of English Painting.* Freeport, NY: Books for Libraries Press, 1969.

Treuherz, Julian. "The Pre-Raphaelites and Medieval Manuscripts." In *The Pre-Raphaelite Papers,* 153–69. London: Tate, 1984.

Tsui, Aileen. "The Phantasm of Aesthetic Autonomy in Whistler's Work: Titling *The White Girl.*" *Art History* 29.3 (June 2006): 444–75.

Tucker, Herbert F., Jr. *Browning's Beginnings.* Minneapolis: University of Minnesota Press, 1980.

———. "From Monomania to Monologue: 'St. Simeon Stylites' and the Rise of the Victorian Dramatic Monologue." *Victorian Poetry,* Special Issue: The Dramatic 'I' Poem, ed. Linda M. Shires, 22.2 (Summer 1984): 121–37.

Turner 1775–1851. Ed. Tate Gallery. London: Idea Books, 1975.

Vadillo, Ana Parejo. *Women Poets and Urban Aestheticism: Passengers of Modernity.* New York: Macmillan, 2005.

Vye, Shelly. "Tourist Geographies: Spectatorship, Space, and Empire in England, 1830–1910." PhD dissertation, Syracuse University, 2004.

Wahrman, Dror. *The Making of the Modern Self: Identity and Culture in Eighteenth-Century England.* New Haven: Yale University Press, 2004.

Warner, Marina, "The Shadow of Young Girls in Flower." Introduction to Virginia Dodier, *Lady Hawarden, Studies From Life 1857–1864,* 6–10. New York: Aperture, 1999.

Welsh, Alexander. *George Eliot and Blackmail.* Cambridge, MA: Harvard University Press, 1985.

Williams, Raymond. *Marxism and Literature.* New York: Oxford University Press, 1977.

Wilton, Andrew. *Painting and Poetry: Turner's Verse Book and His Work of 1804–1812.* London: Tate, 1990.

Winter, Alison. *Mesmerized: Powers of Mind in Victorian Britain.* Chicago: University of Chicago Press, 2000.

Witemeyer, Hugh. *George Eliot and the Visual Arts.* New Haven: Yale University Press, 1979.

Wolf, Bryan Jay. *Vermeer and the Invention of Seeing.* Chicago: University of Chicago Press, 2001.

Wolfson, Susan. *Formal Charges: The Shaping of Poetry in British Romanticism.* Stanford: Stanford University Press, 1999.

Yeazell, Ruth. "Hardy's Rural Painting of the Dutch School." In *Thomas Hardy Reappraised: Essays in Honour of Michael Millgate.* Ed. Keith Wilson, 136–53. Toronto: University of Toronto Press, 2006.

Žižek, Slavoj. *Looking Awry: An Introduction to Jacques Lacan through Popular Culture.* Cambridge, MA: MIT Press, 1992.

VICTORIAN CRITICAL INTERVENTIONS
Donald E. Hall, Series Editor

Included in this series are provocative, theory-based forays into some of the most heated discussions in Victorian studies today, with the goal of redefining what we both know and do in this field.